Praise for
Hell? Yes!

"In *Hell? Yes!* Robert Jeffress approaches the Goliath-like issues of our time with the calm, dead-eye aim of a contemporary David. If you want an encounter with the truth, read this book! It is so timely for this generation."

—JOSH D. MCDOWELL, author and speaker

"Anytime someone is bold enough to tell the outrageous truth, I am ready to listen. Dr. Jeffress holds nothing back in an all-out assault on the lies of Satan, the gates of hell, and the kingdom of darkness. You can plunge into this volume with absolute confidence in the author's fearless fidelity. Join him as he defends seven controversial but essential truths for our times."

—JERRY FALWELL, chancellor of Liberty University

"Robert Jeffress does a superb job of exposing politically incorrect lies that many Americans have embraced and integrated into their lives. He affirms and challenges all of us to use the plumb line of Scripture as our guide to the critical issues impacting our faith and our families. I have the privilege of seeing hundreds of manuscripts and new books each year; *Hell? Yes!* is one text that all Christians should read."

—DR. RICHARD LAND, president of the Southern Baptist
Convention's Ethics and Religious Liberty Commission

"Robert Jeffress is a true hero. So many today are afraid to speak the truth on the key controversial issues of our day…won't take the 'risk' of going after these deceptions head-on…. The truth will set you free."

—MR. KELLY SHACKELFORD, ESQ., chief counsel,
Liberty Legal Institute

"Dr. Robert Jeffress's *Hell? Yes!* is a most provocative work. Whether or not a person agrees with each statement, the book contains many profound truths that should be read by every Christian today."

—D. JAMES KENNEDY, PhD, senior minister of Coral Ridge
Presbyterian Church, Fort Lauderdale

"In *Hell? Yes!* Dr. Jeffress has once again proved his mettle in taking on the difficult subjects.... This book will answer the questions of the mind while it comforts the soul."

—PAIGE PATTERSON, president of Southwestern Baptist
Theological Seminary

I have no doubt that many will come to a place of hope and will find peace for their souls as they read *Hell? Yes!*"

—DENNIS JERNIGAN, author, song writer, and Doxology
recording artist

"*Hell? Yes!* is a book that tackles the tough issues of the day. If you want to dialogue with the culture in a persuasive manner, this is a must-read."

—BOB RECCORD, president of North American Mission Board

"*Hell? Yes!* is refreshing, affirming, and convicting...a must-read for people of every persuasion, but especially for Christians who want to be found faithful in this generation. I intend to recommend this book everywhere I go."

—RICK SCARBOROUGH, president of Vision America

"This is not a book for the weak-willed or the faint of heart. It is a clarion call to stand up for the truth and do something about it."

—DR. ED HINDSON, dean of the Institute of Biblical
Studies, Liberty University

ROBERT JEFFRESS

Hell?
Yes!

...AND OTHER **OUTRAGEOUS** TRUTHS
YOU CAN **STILL** BELIEVE

WATERBROOK
PRESS

HELL? YES!
PUBLISHED BY WATERBROOK PRESS
2375 Telstar Drive, Suite 160
Colorado Springs, Colorado 80920
A division of Random House, Inc.

ISBN 1-57856-520-0

Published in association with Yates & Yates, LLP, Attorneys and Counselors, Orange, California.

Library of Congress Cataloging-in-Publication Data

Jeffress, Robert, 1955–.
Hell? yes! : and other outrageous truths you can still believe / Robert Jeffress.—1st ed.
    p. cm.
  ISBN 1-57856-520-0
  1. Christianity—Miscellanea. 2. Theology, Doctrinal—Miscellanea. I. Title.
BR121.3.J45 2004
239—dc22   2004002959

Printed in the United States of America
2004

10 9 8 7 6 5 4 3 2

To Mrs. W. A. Criswell—
For more than seventy years you have faithfully taught
the immutable truths of God's inerrant Word.
Thank you for the eternal impact your ministry has made on me,
the thousands of members of First Baptist Church, Dallas,
and the tens of thousands who listen by radio
to your Spirit-filled lessons every Sunday morning.

Contents

Acknowledgments

I want to express my deepest appreciation to those who have assisted me in the production of this book...

To Steve Cobb, Don Pape, and the team at WaterBrook Press for your enthusiasm for this project from the very beginning and for your continued encouragement in my writing ministry.

To Bruce Nygren, my editor, for your insightful comments and suggestions.

To my agent and friend, Sealy Yates, for providing your wise counsel throughout this process.

To Bobb Biehl for coming up with the title for this book in less than three minutes over breakfast one morning.

To Cecil Price for your assistance in providing much of the technical research for this project.

To David Barton whose excellent books provided the foundation for much of the material in the chapter titled "America Is a Christian Nation."

To my assistant, Carrilyn Baker, for your help in ways too numerous to enumerate.

And finally, to the members of First Baptist Church, Wichita Falls, for the privilege of serving as your pastor. For twelve years you have never wavered in your love and support for me, even as our church has faced relentless attacks for voicing the "outrageous" truths presented in this book.

Wimp-Free Christianity

"Truth is abhorred by the masses," cautioned the seventeenth-century Jesuit priest Baltasar Gracian. If you don't accept that observation, try making any one of the following comments around the break room at work, or even in the Sunday-school room at church:

- "Only Christians will go to heaven; everyone else is going to hell."
- "The husband is the head of the family."
- "Homosexuality is a perversion."

Then just sit back and watch the fireworks explode! You'll most likely hear the terms *intolerant, bigot, uneducated,* and *arrogant* hurled at you (and those are just some of the nicer words you can expect). By the way, don't be surprised if you hear such harsh judgments coming just as frequently and forcefully from the lips of Christians as from non-Christians. In increasing numbers believers are either abandoning or holding much less tightly to the truths that have been historically embraced by Christians.

Such a charge certainly demands support, so let me offer some from both personal experience and statistical evidence. First, my story.

Big Stink in a Small Town

I pastor a large church in a medium-size town, right in the center of the Bible belt, two hours away from Dallas, Texas, which has been described by *Christianity Today* as the new "Mecca" of evangelical Christianity. A few years ago a member of our church brought me copies of two children's books from our local library: *Daddy's Roommate* and *Heather Has Two Mommies*. Both books tell the story of a child being raised by a homosexual couple. In *Daddy's Roommate,* a young boy's parents divorce so that "Daddy" can live with his homosexual lover, Frank. The little boy is understandably perplexed by the relationship and asks his mother about his father's new "friend." The mother gently explains that "being gay is just one more kind of love" and that "Daddy and his roommate are very happy together."[1] When the little boy asks what Daddy and Frank do, Mom explains that Daddy and Frank live together, eat together, and sleep together. Each activity the mother explains is accompanied by a drawing, including one showing Daddy and Frank together in bed.[2]

It just so happened that the week the books were brought to my attention, my sermon—part of a series on the book of Genesis—was on God's destruction of Sodom and Gomorrah. One of the applications I made at the close of the message was that no society can afford to condone what God has condemned and that there comes a time when Christians need to take a stand against evil. I read from *Daddy's Roommate* and focused on the picture of two men in bed together. "Here is a library book—purchased with your tax dollars—promoting sodomy, which is illegal in the state of Texas, is largely responsible for one of the deadliest epidemics in history (AIDS), and is an abomination to God.... It is time for God's people to say, 'Enough!'"

I explained that I had already spoken with the librarian about removing the books, but she had refused to do so. So I asked our church to petition the city council to remove the books. To make it easier for the city council, I also decided not to return the books to the library so that the council's decision would be whether or not to repurchase the books I was keeping. (I later wrote a check to the library to cover the cost of the books.)

I could never have imagined the firestorm that ignited as a result of that message. Media outlets including the *New York Times,* Associated Press, NBC television, ABC radio, and Rush Limbaugh carried the story. PBS sent a crew to Wichita Falls and filmed a documentary on the furor that divided our city. I was fervently denounced by the American Civil Liberties Union (ACLU), People for the American Way (PFAW), the American Library Association (ALA), and Americans United for Separation of Church and State (which later threatened our church's tax-exempt status). The editor of the local newspaper wrote an editorial condemning me for promoting censorship and suggesting that I should be jailed for my act of civil disobedience.

When we eventually persuaded the city council to pass a compromise regulation giving three hundred adults the right to request that a book deemed offensive be moved from the children's area to the adult section of the library, the ACLU filed suit in federal court to overturn the council's action. According to some legal experts, the ACLU won that challenge, not because the regulation itself was unconstitutional, but because the council's actions were influenced by people of faith.

But what surprised me most during that two-year ordeal was the reaction of many Christians to our church's stand against homosexuality. One prominent minister of a large denominational church in our community stood in his pulpit one Sunday during the furor and said that *he* was "not called upon to judge, but to tell others about love." A letter to the editor of the *Times Record News* several days later praised the open-minded pastor:

> Hurray for Dr. _____.... None of us are here to judge and those who choose to actively seek to influence others should do so

in a positive manner. We have enough trouble already with hatred
and intolerance. Churches have too long been a place where
people go to elevate themselves above others, to look down their
noses in disdain at the rest of the world. These people have ruined
the meaning of the word "worship."... Pastors such as Jeffress who
have such hatred in their hearts toward any group or individual
should be immediately dismissed from any position of influence.... I urge the congregation of First Baptist Church to replace
Jeffress with a kinder, more compassionate pastor.[3]

Apparently the letter writer's tolerance and compassion extend to
everyone except pastors who don't share her viewpoint. Other Christians piled on charges of intolerance, bigotry, hatred, or simply poor
judgment in causing a division in our community by taking on a "political" issue. Most alarmingly, when these Christians were reminded of
the biblical teaching on homosexuality, common replies included:

- "Those prohibitions were unique to the culture then, but they
  don't apply today."
- "Science has taught us a lot about homosexuality since the
  Bible was written."
- "That may be what *we* believe, but not everyone accepts the
  Bible."

Of course, all of those responses beg the same question: Are there
absolute truths that apply to all people at all times, regardless of their
faith—or lack of faith?

THE RISE OF RELATIVISM

Recent surveys tell us that the majority of both Christians and non-
Christians answer that question with a resounding "No!" Researcher

George Barna already knew that only a minority of both Christians and non-Christians believed in moral absolutes that transcended time and culture. One would think the terrorist attacks on September 11, 2001, which were almost universally denounced as evil, would increase the number of people believing in moral absolutes. In reality, the opposite occurred. A survey conducted in the aftermath of the attacks revealed that *fewer* Americans accepted the notion of absolute truth than prior to September 11. By a 3-to-1 margin, adults said that truth is always relative to a person's individual situation. This view was even more prevalent among teenagers—only 6 percent believed that there is such a thing as absolute moral truth.[4]

But surely the statistics would be different among Christians who would naturally regard the Bible as the source of absolute truth, right? Don't be so sure. Barna's survey revealed that 68 percent of born-again adults and 91 percent of born-again teenagers rejected the concept of absolute truth.[5]

Now you can understand why the three incendiary statements mentioned at the beginning of this chapter are guaranteed to illicit such a negative reaction not only from unbelievers but from professing Christians as well. We have bought into the concept of relative truth, a concept that is best explained by the simple dictum "Everything is right sometime, and nothing is right every time."

It's no wonder, Barna notes, that substantial numbers of Christians believe that activities such as homosexuality, cohabitation, and pornography are permissible in some circumstances. "Without some firm and compelling basis for suggesting that such acts are inappropriate, people are left with philosophies such as 'if it feels good, do it.'"[6] Or as another writer says, "Being good is now defined as feeling good."

But the fallout from the wholesale rejection of absolute truth (which, as we will see later, is really just a replacement of one set of absolutes for another) is not confined to morality. The all-out war against absolute truth in favor of relative truth explains why people bristle when someone says, "Jesus Christ is the only way to heaven," "America is a Christian nation," or "Abortion is murder." The greatest sin in our culture today is to claim to be right about *anything*. Author Allan Bloom, in his book *The Closing of the American Mind,* writes,

> The study of history and of culture teaches that all the world was mad in the past; men always thought they were right, and that led to wars, persecutions, slavery, xenophobia, racism, and chauvinism. The point is not to correct the mistakes and really be right; rather it is not to think you are right at all.[7]

So what? you may wonder. While we may sigh and shake our heads over our culture's rejection of absolute truth, what real difference does it make in our lives? Let me cite just three of many ramifications that occur when a society embraces relativism (the rejection of absolute truth).

1. Relativism encourages immorality. This is the most obvious result of jettisoning the concept of absolute truth—and it will eventually touch your family. For example, if there are no moral absolutes, then why shouldn't *all* sexual activity be permitted, including pedophilia (sex between adults and children)? "But," you may say, "that's different because it involves an adult forcing a child to have sex. Coercion in sex is wrong."

Yet if there are no absolute moral principles that transcend time and culture, who has the right to say that the rape of a child is wrong? The relativist will answer, "Society has the right to formulate its own standards of morality, and in our society we have decided that pedophilia is wrong."

May I remind you that only forty years ago society deemed homosexuality a psychological aberration and outlawed homosexual practice in most states. Yet today it is generally accepted—even among Christians—that while homosexuality may be wrong, every person has a right to choose his or her own sexual behavior.

Forty years from now we may hear the same arguments for legitimizing pedophilia that have been so successful in normalizing homosexuality:

- "Pedophiles do not *choose* pedophilia; they are born that way."
- "Why force pedophiles to hide their sexuality and live in shame?"
- "Don't pedophiles have a right to happiness through the full expression of their sexuality?"

This possibility is not as far-fetched as it first appears. Carson Holloway, a political science professor at the University of Nebraska, claims that a growing movement toward normalizing pedophilia is the latest manifestation of the trend toward discarding moral absolutes. In a lecture presented at the Family Research Council on July 10, 2002, Professor Holloway discussed how our nation's standard for morality has digressed to the point where "anything sexual is morally permissible, so long as it takes place between 'consenting adults.' "[8] But Holloway has strong reason to believe such a standard is fluid. Why deny a twelve- or thirteen-year-old child the right to "consent" to sex with an adult? Those who defend pedophilia claim that children today are "so much more worldly-wise about these matters…that they can, in some cases, be the instigators of intergenerational sexual activity."[9]

This trend toward normalizing pedophilia can be seen in the decision of the United States Supreme Court in April 2002 that permitted the distribution and possession of virtual child pornography. The Court reasoned that the federal statute prohibiting virtual child pornography did not apply if the pornography had social, political, scientific, or cultural value.[10] In essence, their ruling followed the lines of the one-man's-pornography-is-another-man's-art argument.

Some psychiatrists are also jumping on the bandwagon to normalize pedophilia. In July 1998 the American Psychological Association's *Psychological Bulletin* published "A Meta-Analytic Examination of Assumed Properties of Child Sexual Abuse Using College Samples" by Bruce Rind, Philip Tromovitch, and Robert Bauserman. The paper contended that sex with a child may not always be harmful to the child as long as the child "enjoys" it. Although the American Psychological Association (APA) did not endorse the paper, Dr. Laura Schlessinger observes that its willingness to publish such a paper without careful scrutiny is a thinly veiled attempt to normalize pedophilia.[11] Although the APA at present has an anti–child molestation policy, what is to keep that policy from changing just as the APA's designation of homosexuality changed to one of acceptance in the 1970s? After all, in a world of no absolutes, any kind of behavior is permissible.

2. Relativism discourages evangelism. Recently I was watching a popular talk show, and the topic was "Is There Only One Way to Heaven?" The host allowed various audience members to voice their predictable complaints that insisting on one way of salvation was arrogant and hateful. However, one poor soul summoned the courage to stand up and say, "My Lord and Savior Jesus Christ said, 'I am the Way, the Truth, and the Life. No man comes to the Father but by Me.'" The host responded, "My dear, I am glad you believe that. You have every right to believe that for yourself. But you have no right to try and coerce me to believe that way."

Notice the two assumptions that undergirded the host's comments. First, the host assumed that Jesus's claim that He is the only Source of salvation applies only to those who choose to believe it! Put another way, truth is truth only to those who choose to accept it as truth. The absurdity of such a premise will be explored further in the next section.

The other assumption is not quite so obvious, but it is extremely dangerous. In the host's mind, voicing your belief in absolute truth is "coercion." To claim that Jesus's words apply to everyone is to engage in intolerant and hateful speech. This assumption leads to another frightening consequence of relativism.

3. Relativism promotes persecution. In a society that rejects absolute truth, the only vice that cannot be tolerated is the sin of intolerance. Thus, those who assert that Jesus Christ is the only way to heaven or that homosexuality is wrong are engaging in hate speech. Why? Because, according to the relativist, such assertions, by inference, mean that the Hindu or the homosexual is inferior and deserving of mistreatment by society. Thus, "hateful" speech must be silenced even if it means violating constitutional rights.

If you think such a statement is overly dramatic, just consider what is happening in Sweden, a country long known for its tolerance of all lifestyles. In May 2002, 56 percent of that nation's lawmakers passed a draft bill that would make pastors who label homosexuality "immoral" subject to prison terms of up to four years. The powerful homosexual lobby in Sweden is pushing for the draft bill to eventually become a constitutional amendment. If the bill becomes law, Sören Andersson, president of the Swedish Federation for Lesbian, Gay, Bisexual and Transgender Rights, pledges to aggressively track down and report "hate speech irrespective of where it occurs."[12] Annalie Enochson, a Swedish parliament member who is also a Christian, predicts the frightening consequences of such a law: "That means people coming from the [homosexual] lobby group could sit in our churches having on the tape recorder and listen to somebody and say, 'What you are saying now is against our constitution.'"[13]

   That kind of persecution is not as far away from our own country as you might think. In Canada, Hugh Owens placed an ad in a newspaper quoting passages from the Bible denouncing homosexuality. Three men filed complaints with the Saskatchewan Human Rights Commission saying that the ad "cut their feelings to the quick" because it contained Bible verses that denounced homosexuality. Owens was fined $4,500 by the commission for engaging in "offensive behavior." You may ask, "But what about Owens's right of free speech?" The commission determined that Owens was permitted to speak out against homosexuality—just as long as he did not cite passages of Scripture. (I promise I'm not making this up.) Disparaging remarks about homosexuals combined with passages from the Bible "expose or tend to expose homosexuals to hatred or ridicule" and are therefore subject to punishment.[14]

   Owens's crime was not that he spoke out against homosexuality, but that by quoting the Bible, he dared to suggest that his statements were more than his personal beliefs and thus were applicable to everyone. That kind of "intolerance" cannot be tolerated and must be silenced, according to the relativist. And the silencing process is beginning in our own nation.

   On May 5, 1995, Judge Samuel B. Kent of the District Court for the Southern District of Texas mandated that any student who dared to mention the name of Jesus Christ in a graduation prayer would be sentenced to six months in jail. Here are the judge's words:

And make no mistake, the court is going to have a United States marshal in attendance at the graduation. If any student offends this court, that student will be summarily arrested and will face up to six months incarceration in the Galveston County Jail for contempt of court. Anyone who thinks I'm kidding about this order...[or] expressing any weakness or lack of resolve in that spirit of compromise would better think again. Anyone who violates these orders, no kidding, is going to wish that he or she had died as a child when this court gets through with it.[15]

How's that for an example of tolerance! Apparently the judge believes that the First Amendment to the United States Constitution, guaranteeing freedom of speech and worship, applies to everyone *except* Christians who pray in Jesus's name. Gracian was right. "Truth is abhorred by the masses."

My primary concern, however, is not with society's rejection of absolute truth, but with the growing number of Christians who are waffling in their convictions regarding some of the basic tenets of the faith. To be blunt, I'm sick and tired of wimpy Christians...and they're all around us. For example:

- A Christian leader is interviewed on a popular talk show and asked whether a moral Muslim is going to hell. He responds, "That's not for me to decide. We must let a good and loving God make that determination."

- A Christian mother is invited to offer a prayer at her PTA meeting and closes her prayer with "In Your name" instead of "In Jesus's name" so as not to offend non-Christians in the audience.

- A Christian serving on the local school board caves in to pressure to reject a science textbook that mentions creationism as an alternative to evolution by reasoning, "Although that is what *I* believe personally, we must respect the separation of church and state."

Instead of boldly holding out the light of truth in "a crooked and perverse generation" (Philippians 2:15), Christians are increasingly hiding or even extinguishing the light of absolute truth in order to blend in with the darkness of the world. George Barna eloquently explains what happens when Christians reject absolute truth and embrace relativism:

> When a majority of Christian adults...proudly cast their vote
> for moral relativism, the Church is in trouble.... The failure
> to address this issue at its root, and to do so quickly and persua-
> sively, will undermine the strength of the Church for at least
> another generation, and probably longer.[16]

What Is Truth?

In the chapters that follow, we are going to examine seven of the most "politically incorrect" truths that I believe Christians need to reclaim in order to once again become the salt and light Jesus exhorts us to be. These truths are routinely denounced and attacked on television talk shows, in high-school and college classrooms, and even in many churches across our nation. Those who dare to make these seven claims will be subjected to social, academic, and even legal persecution. Yet, in spite of the venomous attacks against these seven "outrageous" truths, we will discover that they are grounded in theological, scientific, and/or historical evidence. Here they are...

1. *Every other religion is wrong.* Regardless of what you hear today, all religions do *not* lead to God. In chapter 1 we will answer the most popular objections to the claim that Jesus Christ is the only Way to God.

2. *God is ultimately responsible for suffering.* Why would a loving God allow famines, earthquakes, terrorist attacks, murders, and deformed babies? If God is all-powerful, why doesn't He stop such horrendous suffering? Even unbelievers understand that when we attempt to let God off the hook for such suffering in the world, we are unintentionally incapacitating the Almighty. In chapter 3 we will discover why God is willing to take ultimate responsibility for everything that happens in His universe.

3. *God sends good people to hell.* Other religions do not only lead people away from the true God, they also lead people to a literal hell. In spite of the wholesale rejection of the concept of hell by non-Christians as well as many Christians, there are strong biblical and philosophical reasons for believing in the reality of a place of eternal torment. We'll explore these arguments in chapter 2.

4. *Homosexuality is a perversion.* Are some people born with a predisposition toward homosexuality? If our sexuality were biologically predetermined, why would we label homosexuality as immoral? In chapter 4 we will explode seven common myths about homosexuality.

5. *Husbands are to be the leaders of their families.* Should the idea of wives submitting to their husbands be relegated to the Stone Age? In chapter 5 we will rediscover what the Bible really says—and doesn't say—about the roles of husbands and wives in marriage.

6. *Evolution is a myth.* Some people claim that evolution's explanation for the origin of life belongs in the classroom, while creationism should be left in the church. In chapter 6 we will

explore both the scientific and theological reasons for rejecting evolution.

7. *America is a Christian nation.* You've probably heard that (1)
   our nation's founders were secularists or deists, not Christians,
   (2) those who came to our country in search of religious freedom came from a variety of religious backgrounds, and (3)
   the separation of church and state is a foundational principle
   of our Constitution. In fact, all of these statements are historically inaccurate, as we will discover in chapter 7.

Why do people today react so violently against the above statements, which, until recently, were generally accepted by a large segment
of the populace? While each one of these statements is guaranteed to
offend some groups, taken together they represent a philosophical point
of view that is in disrepute today: the notion of absolute truth. The late
Ray Stedman gave a simple definition of absolute truth: "Truth is reality, the way things really are."

But is it possible to define "the way things really are"? And if it *is*
possible, how do we go about discovering that reality? For nearly seventeen hundred years, the Bible was viewed by many as the source of
absolute truth. During the Age of Reason, however, the modernist (or
rationalist) replaced the religionist as the judge of truth. "Reality can be
discovered through investigation. Only what can be observed and measured is real," the modernist claimed. Thus, science replaced the Bible
as the arbiter of truth. Only what was scientifically verifiable could be
labeled "true."

While modernists rejected the supernatural claims of the Bible
because they could not be observed, at least modernists and Christians
had one thing in common: They believed in the concept of truth,
though they differed on how that truth was discovered. Modernists

found reality through the microscope, while Christians discovered reality through the Bible. Yet, although they did not agree on the *content* of truth, they were in agreement on the *concept* of truth.

However, the age in which we live today rejects even the concept of absolute truth. Instead, *truth* is whatever an individual or society determines it to be. For example, our society may decide that euthanasia (the killing of those who are hopelessly ill to prevent their continued suffering) is wrong. Yet a country wracked with the AIDS epidemic may permit euthanasia for the well-being of individuals and society. Who is right? Today, many—often called postmodernists—say there is no absolute right or wrong. It depends on the situation. Remember the maxim "Everything is right sometime, and nothing is right every time"?

You can see how such thinking impacts Christianity. Today non-Christians—whether or not they are familiar with the term *postmodern*—are no longer trying to determine whether Christianity is "right," but whether "it is right *for me*." When a Christian shares his or her faith with an unbeliever, instead of a vociferous objection to the truth claims of Christianity, the more likely response is, "I'm glad that works for you, but I'm searching for my own truth."

The reason for this brief philosophical explanation is to help you understand why many people react so violently to the seven claims we will discuss in this book. The postmodern thinker or relativist says, "If Jesus Christ is your Savior, fine, but don't try to force that belief on me. If you believe that homosexuality is wrong, I have no argument with that, but don't say it is wrong for everyone." Again, the greatest sin to a postmodernist is claiming to be right about *anything*.

This book, however, is built upon the philosophical foundation of absolute truth, or as the late Francis Schaeffer called it, "true truth." These theological, sociological, scientific, and historical realities apply to everyone at every time, regardless of individual or societal preferences. These seven claims are built on three premises concerning absolute truth:

1. *Absolute truth is universal.* Once, while listening to a talk-radio program, I heard a perfect example of how even Christians have unwittingly embraced the postmodern concept of relative truth. The debate was over displaying the Ten Commandments in public schools. The conversation went something like this:

CALLER: We have a responsibility to post these commandments in the schools since they apply not only to Christians but to everyone. God said He would bless any nation that keeps these commandments and judge any nation that disregards them.

RADIO HOST: I'm a Christian, and I agree with you. These commands do apply to everyone, but not everyone believes like you and I do.

CALLER: But that's the point! The commands *do* apply to everyone, regardless of whether or not they accept them.

RADIO HOST: But don't you understand? *We* believe that, but not everyone does.

On and on the discussion went. Do you see the philosophical conflict? The Christian radio host, voicing the relativist's point of view, believes that the universal applicability of the Ten Commandments applies only to those who *believe* in the universal applicability of the Ten Commandments. That would be like saying the law of gravity applies only to those who believe in the law of gravity. If someone jumps out of an airplane without a parachute, his fate is certain regardless of whether or not he believes in the reality of gravity.

By the way, everyone believes in absolute truth, whether or not one realizes it. Let me illustrate what I mean. The person who claims that there are no absolute truths is guilty of asserting an absolute truth! She is making the absolute judgment that nowhere in the universe are there truths that are applicable to everyone. How can she make that claim with such certainty?

In his book *The New Absolutes,* William Watkins argues that instead of rejecting absolute truth, relativists are simply replacing old truths with new truths. For example, an old truth was that life began at conception and should be protected. That truth is being replaced by a new "truth": A woman has a right to choose what happens to her own body. Since the relativist believes this right belongs to everyone, he is declaring an absolute truth.

An old truth was that the propagation of Christianity was good for America. That truth has been replaced with the new truth that all religion should be banned from the public square and that government should always be neutral (translation: hostile) toward Christianity. That's a new absolute truth.

An old truth was that in issues of morality, there were definite rights and wrongs. But that old truth has been replaced by a new truth: Instead of judging, we should tolerate behavior we find objectionable.

The irony of what my friend Josh McDowell calls the "new tolerance" is best expressed by philosophy professor Leslie Armour: "Our idea is that to be a virtuous citizen is to be one who tolerates everything except intolerance."[17] Or, as one public-school administrator said, "It is the mission of public schools not to tolerate intolerances."[18] The relativist fails to see (or acknowledge) that to label intolerance as "evil" is to make an absolute statement.

My point is painfully obvious: Everyone believes in absolute truth. The only question is, *Which* absolute truths will you accept? And this leads to a second observation.

2. Absolute truth is revealed. Through the years many have disagreed with President George W. Bush's tough stance against Iraq, North Korea, the Taliban, and other oppressive regimes. After all, some ask, what gives the United States the right to impose its values on others? Fair question.

In his book *Bush at War,* Bob Woodward reveals what has motivated the president to intervene on behalf of those who are suffering starvation, torture, and prison brutality under totalitarian societies. It is Bush's belief in absolute truth, which the president expressed this way in an interview with Woodward:

> There is a human condition that we must worry about in times
> of war. There is a value system that cannot be compromised—
> God-given values. These aren't United States–created values.
> There are values of freedom and the human condition and moth-
> ers loving their children. What's very important as we articulate
> foreign policy through our diplomacy and military action, is that
> it never look like we are creating—we are the author of these
> values. It leads to a larger question of your view about God.[19]

The relativist believes that truth is constructed by individuals and society. Since no two people and no two societies are alike, the relativist rejects the one-truth-fits-all notion. Thus, when he is pressed, the relativist cannot make a logical argument against a government's choosing to starve and torture its citizens. After all, who says such actions are wrong? One college professor has expressed his dream of a liberal utopia based on the premise that cruelty toward one's fellow man is the greatest offense. But being a moral relativist, he admits that he cannot prove why cruelty is the greatest sin in the world or, for that matter, a sin at all. He admits that this "moral law" is based on his own preference. Adolf Hitler's vision of utopia was based on an entirely different principle: the elimination of the Jewish race and all other non-Aryan races. In a world without absolute truths, who has the right to label the professor's vision "good" and Hitler's version "evil"?

Everyone believes in absolute truth. The question is how we derive that truth. President Bush—and millions of others—believe that truth is not formulated by individuals; rather, it is received by individuals from a Higher Source. Man's responsibility is not to develop truth, but to discover it.

Where is this truth to be found? For two thousand years Christians have believed that the Bible is the repository of God's eternal, nonnegotiable truths. While there are sound philosophical, scientific, sociological, and historical reasons for accepting the seven controversial truths we will explore in this book, ultimately they are all built on the presupposition that the Bible is God's perfect and complete message to humankind.

The evidence for believing that the Bible is such a book goes beyond the scope of this volume. However, may I suggest that if you struggle with this issue—or know someone who does—you might consider reading the excellent book *Seven Reasons You Can Trust the Bible* by Dr. Erwin Lutzer. Dr. Lutzer simply and forcefully explains the historical, scientific, and archaeological evidence for accepting the Bible as God's perfect and complete revelation.

3. Absolute truth is exclusive. In a sincere effort to promote harmony during an argument, someone might say, "Well, perhaps we are *both* right." In a relativistic culture it is much more acceptable to say "we're both right" than to claim "I'm right and you're wrong." But if there is such a thing as absolute truth, then it only follows that there are also absolute untruths. Why do we find it so difficult to label certain ideas or values as wrong?

I believe it is because we have confused the concepts of *diversity* and *pluralism.* Diversity is the acknowledgment that there are a variety of opinions. For example, we must acknowledge that there are thousands of religions in the world. However, pluralism goes one step further and says that given the diversity of beliefs, no one belief system can claim to be "right."

Yet the person who accepts the notion of absolute truth must logically be willing to label some beliefs as wrong. For example, author R. C. Sproul, recalling the Senate hearings in which Anita Hill accused Supreme Court Justice Clarence Thomas of sexual harassment, confessed that he wasn't sure who was lying and who was telling the truth. But he was absolutely sure that "they both couldn't be telling the truth."[20]

Similarly, not all religions can be telling the truth about God and man. For example, Christianity claims that eternal salvation is received as a gift from God, while Islam claims that salvation is earned through good deeds. While it is possible that Christianity and Islam are both wrong, it is impossible for both of them to be right. If Islam is right, then Christianity is wrong, and vice versa. Absolute truth by definition rejects other truth claims.

Yet there is a difference between rejecting beliefs and rejecting the people who hold those beliefs. Unfortunately, the pages of history are filled with examples of Christians who have used their grasp of the truth as a club with which to oppress, persecute, and marginalize others. In the final chapter of this book, I will discuss how Christians can stay on the offensive with their beliefs without being offensive to others.

Nevertheless, we cannot allow the abuses of some to push us into what one writer refers to as a "forced neutrality" in which we dare not express any idea that might offend another person. Instead, as William Watkins writes, it is time for a renewed intolerance:

> We must violate the new tolerance and become people marked by intolerance. Not an intolerance that unleashes hate upon people, but an intolerance that's unwilling to allow error to masquerade as truth. An intolerance that calls evil *evil* and good *good.*[21]

If you are weary of a watered-down version of Christianity that wavers and waffles about controversial issues; if you are tired of dodging some of the hard questions that non-Christian friends, neighbors, or work associates ask; if you are ready and willing to stand up and compassionately, but forcefully and intelligently, proclaim, "This is what I believe…and here's why," then you are going to enjoy our time together in the pages that follow.

Every Other Religion
Is Wrong

s there a chance I could get out on your first flight in the morning?"
I asked hopefully. Having wrapped up my interviews early, I was anxious to get home after visiting three cities in four days to promote my latest book.

"No problem," the agent assured me. "We have a flight leaving in the morning at nine o'clock, and it is wide open."

The next morning I awakened at 5:00 in order to arrive at the airport early enough to be first on the standby list. After going through the security checks and gulping down a Starbucks grande latte and muffin, I waited expectantly for my name to be called.

"We're sorry, Dr. Jeffress, but another flight canceled, and this one is now oversold," the gate agent informed me. "But we do have another flight leaving at 11:00 a.m."

I dutifully went to the new departure gate, placed my name on the list, and once again watched another plane pull back from the gate without me. The agent apologized but assured me that the 1:00 p.m. flight looked great.

Like a lemming, I walked to the new gate and once again experienced the same fate. Finally, after seven hours of waiting, hoping, and counting passengers, I was allowed to board a plane—the one on which I had originally been booked.

No sooner had I plopped down in my aisle seat and pulled out the in-flight magazine than my seatmate began to talk.

"What line of work are you in?" he inquired.

How I answer that question always depends on whether or not I'm in the mood to converse. If I have a briefcase full of work and want to limit the chitchat, I reply, "I'm a pastor." If I *really* don't want to talk, I answer, "I'm a *Southern Baptist* preacher." Trust me, that is always a conversation stopper.

But this time I sensed that I should talk with my traveling companion. Perhaps my inability to secure a seat on an earlier flight was part of a divine plan. So I answered, "I'm a writer."

"What kind of books do you write?" he probed.

"Christian books," I answered tentatively, wondering if that reply would end our dialogue.

"That's interesting. I used to be a Christian but gave it up," he admitted.

For the next four hours as we winged our way from Seattle to Dallas, my fellow passenger explained to me why he was no longer a believer. Doubts about the Bible, unanswered prayers, and the breakup of his marriage were all reasons for his departure from the faith. But his underlying objection to Christianity is what we spent the bulk of our time discussing: "I cannot believe that Jesus Christ is the only way to God, because if that is true, then the majority of people in the world are going to hell. I can't believe in a God who would be that intolerant."

In those two sentences my seatmate articulated the single greatest objection to Christianity—what is really the mother of all politically incorrect statements: "Jesus Christ is the only way to God, and therefore, every other religion in the world is wrong."

Is There Only One Way to Heaven?

If you are a regular viewer of the shouting-head cable-news programs, then you know that anytime a Christian conservative is interviewed, the interviewer will at some point hit her with this line of questioning: "Are you saying that your way is the only way to God?" The guest will usually make clear that it isn't "her way" but "God's way" to heaven that she is proclaiming. However, that distinction is not enough to prevent the interviewer or other guests from pounding the Christian with every kind of charge imaginable. Just read the following exchange from an episode of *Donahue* in which Phil Donahue interviewed a Baptist theologian (Dr. Albert Mohler), a Jewish Christian (Michael Brown), and a Jewish rabbi (Rabbi Shmuley Boteach).

DONAHUE: Did Gandhi go to heaven?

BROWN: I'm not Gandhi's judge, but if Gandhi rejected Jesus, he's not good enough to get in. You're not good enough, I'm not good enough. We need help. We need salvation....

DONAHUE: But you're telling Jews they're not going to heaven.

BROWN: I'm telling Hindus, I'm telling gentiles, I'm telling Catholics, I'm telling Protestants...

BOTEACH: He's an equal-opportunity offender. You know, if Jesus were alive today, I think he would take Reverend Mohler and Dr. Brown to court for character assassination. They took the prince of peace and made him into the torturer in chief. They took someone who was supposed to redeem, you know, the world, and made him someone who demeans mankind. They have made Jesus into someone who sits in the heavens as some sort of blackmailer in chief—I'm going to torture you, fry you in a wok, murder you, all because you don't believe in me, irrespective of how you behave, Phil. And that's an abomination.

Later in the broadcast Phil Donahue lectured Dr. Brown, the Jewish Christian, for "trying to convert all your Jewish friends to Christianity." Brown explained that telling others about his faith is part of the mandate of Christianity. Donahue then cut to the chase with this comment:

> DONAHUE: You can tell me about it. But you can't stand there righteously and tell me you know what's good for me. And you sure as hell can't tell me that there's only one way for me to get to heaven. Nobody is that smart, nobody.[1]

What is it about Christianity's claim of exclusivity that causes people like my seatmate to reject the faith and a talk-show host's blood to boil? Why will a Christian always be labeled as either an unenlightened schmuck (at best) or a rabid bigot (at worst) for simply adhering to one of the most historic tenets of Christianity?

To be fair, let's lay out the common objections to those who insist that faith in Christ is the only way to reach heaven:

1. *"You are being intolerant."* The greatest evil in today's culture is not theft, rape, or murder. It is intolerance. As we saw in the introduction, people are willing to tolerate any viewpoint, except one that claims to be uniquely true. Recently a dean at Stanford University started pressuring evangelical Christian groups on the campus to stop "proselytizing other students." What so angered the dean was not the content being shared with other students, but the practice of sharing it. Why? Because when a Christian approaches a non-Christian with the gospel, the implication is that the Christian's beliefs are superior—the Christian, ipso facto, is guilty of the unpardonable sin of intolerance.[2]

A number of years ago, my grandmother wrote a widely published poem titled "A Plea for Tolerance." But the way my grandmother understood tolerance and the manner in which it is being defined today are vastly different. In his book *The New Tolerance,* Josh McDowell points out that tolerance used to be a synonym for respect—"Even though I may not agree with you, I respect your right to believe as you do." Every American citizen, as well as every Christian, should embrace that kind of tolerance. One of the foundational principles of our nation has been every citizen's right to choose his or her own religion—or no religion. That freedom is based on God's willingness to grant His creatures the freedom to serve Him.

Today, however, the definition of *tolerance* has undergone a radical transformation. Thomas Helmbock, executive vice president of the national Lambda Chi Alpha fraternity writes, "The definition of new… tolerance is that every individual's beliefs, values, lifestyle, and perception of truth claims are equal.… There is no hierarchy of truth. Your beliefs and my beliefs are equal, and all truth is relative."[3]

You can see this redefinition of *tolerance* demonstrated in our nation's judiciary. One judge for the Sixth Circuit Court of Appeals claims that not only should adherents of all faiths enjoy equal rights as citizens (who would quibble with that?) but "all faiths are equally valid as religions."[4] Unfortunately, the slippery slope of tolerance leads to such illogical conclusions.

For example, suppose a teacher returns to her students the semester exams she has graded over the weekend. One of the students answers every question correctly, except question number ten: "What is the capital of New York?" His answer, "New York City," is marked incorrect. When he challenges the teacher, she reminds him that the correct answer is Albany. But he is not satisfied. He turns to his classmates and asks, "How many of you thought the capital of New York was New York City?" Half the students in the class raise their hands. The student then turns to the teacher and says, "So what makes you think your opinion is more valid than our opinion? You're being intolerant. Aren't all opinions equally valid?" Obviously, there is only one right answer to that question regardless of how many incorrect opinions exist.

But now let's suppose that the same student says to the teacher, "I think it is too hot in here. Would you turn down the thermostat?" The teacher says, "The temperature is just right; we'll leave it where it is." Whose opinion is correct? Obviously, both opinions are equally valid since there is no objective standard for the "right" temperature.

Most major religions attempt to answer the question "How can a person have a right relationship with God?" But our culture is attempting to move the answer to that question from the arena of objective truth (such as state capitals) to the arena of opinion (such as comfortable temperatures). This means that anyone who tries to shift answers from the realm of opinion back to the realm of objective truth will be regarded as being just as intolerant as a person who tries to impose his opinions about the temperature, music, or politics on others.

2. "Exclusivity promotes hatred." According to some, the claim that your religion provides the only way to God promotes not only intolerance but also hatred of those who do not share your beliefs. Consider the words of Rabbi Boteach during an exchange with Larry King:

> I am absolutely against any religion that says that one faith is superior to another. I don't see how that is anything different than spiritual racism. It's a way of saying that we are closer to God than you, and that's what leads to hatred.[5]

Those who object to the idea of absolute truth in general, and to the exclusive claims of Christianity in particular, claim that the my-way-is-the-only-way belief has been responsible for some of the greatest atrocities in human history, including the Crusades and the Holocaust.

Therefore, as Allan Bloom explained, the highest ideal is no longer the discovery of truth, but disabusing yourself and others of the notion that there is a truth to be discovered (see the introduction).

Why is this reluctance to affirm absolute truth a virtue? Why has the quest for tolerance replaced the quest for truth as the highest ideal? Because of the unquestioned assumption that absolute truth leads to hatred and oppression. That assumption is already widely accepted today in the academic world. For example, several months after the terrorist attacks of September 11, 2001, former president Bill Clinton addressed the students at Georgetown University and partly blamed the attacks on America's "arrogant self-righteousness." If only both sides could realize that there is no such thing as absolute truth, perhaps this catastrophe could have been avoided, Clinton suggested. "Nobody's got the truth.... You're at a university which basically believes that no one ever has the whole truth, ever.... We are incapable of ever having the whole truth."[6]

This demonization of those who claim absolute truth has spilled over into the world of evangelical Christianity. One Gallup poll revealed that 88 percent of evangelical Christians believe that the "Bible is the written word of God and is totally accurate in all it teaches." Yet, of those same evangelicals, 53 percent claimed that there are no absolute truths![7] Why? They have accepted hook, line, and sinker the assumption that exclusivity promotes hatred.

But is that contention logical? Imagine that your child develops a terrible cough and fever. You try the usual medications, but nothing works. Your child becomes increasingly listless as you become increasingly worried. You take your child to the doctor, and your physician says, "Your child has pneumonia, and I want to hospitalize her so that she can be watched and treated with antibiotics."

However, you strongly object, saying, "I don't believe my child has pneumonia."

Your doctor explains that there is no question about the diagnosis and needed treatment. But you counter, "Why do you think your opinion is better than mine?"

The doctor patiently responds that as a professional he routinely deals with cases just like this, and the only way to treat the illness is with a heavy round of antibiotics. He insists that he is right (meaning you are wrong). Is it fair to label your doctor as "hateful" or "arrogant" because he argues that there is only one way for your child to get well?

Obviously, our culture's de facto acceptance that exclusivity translates into hatred is seriously flawed.

3. *"How can so many people be wrong?"* This objection to the exclusive claims of Christianity has special appeal to those in a Western culture who routinely assume that the minority is usually wrong and the majority must be right. Charles Templeton, a former preaching colleague of Billy Graham who later became an agnostic, summarized the argument this way:

> Christians are a small minority in the world. Approximately four of every five people on the face of the earth believe in gods other than the Christian God. The more than five billion people who live on earth revere or worship more than three hundred gods. If one includes the animist or tribal religions, that number rises to more than three thousand. Are we to believe that only Christians are right?[8]

Let me help Templeton make his point even more forcefully. According to the *World Christian Encyclopedia,* of the nearly 6 billion people on our planet, there are more than 1 billion Muslims, more than 650 million Hindus, more than 300 million Buddhists, and more than 200 million followers of Chinese folk religions. Only about 25 percent of the world's population would even claim to be Christians (1.6 billion), with the number of true followers of Christ being much less, if we are to take seriously Jesus's words that many who profess to be Christ-followers are actually lost (see Matthew 7:13-23).

How can so many sincere, religious people be wrong? And are we to believe that if they are wrong, God would send them to hell simply because they are mistaken in their beliefs?

Later in this chapter we will examine what the Bible says about the exclusive nature of the gospel and how to present those truth claims to non-Christians. But in reference to this specific objection, it is important to note that Jesus Christ predicted that the majority of the world's population would not go to heaven:

> Enter through the narrow gate; for the gate is wide and the way
> is broad that leads to destruction, and there are many who enter
> through it. For the gate is small and the way is narrow that leads
> to life, and there are few who find it. (Matthew 7:13-14)

Admittedly, it is jarring to think that the vast majority of people will spend eternity in hell. But even more jolting is the realization that many of those who will be in hell are religious people who mistakenly think they are destined for heaven. In the very same passage, Jesus said,

> Not everyone who says to Me, "Lord, Lord," will enter the king-
> dom of heaven, but he who does the will of My Father who is in
> heaven will enter. Many will say to Me on that day, "Lord, Lord,

did we not prophesy in Your name, and in Your name cast out
demons, and in Your name perform many miracles?" And then
I will declare to them, "I never knew you; Depart from Me, you
who practice lawlessness." (Matthew 7:21-23)

Many opponents of Christianity believe they win their argument
against the exclusivity of the gospel by pointing out the obvious conclusion that if Christianity is true and every other religion is wrong,
then the majority of people will go to hell. The critics' desired response
from their listeners is, "Oh, that's too horrible to be true. Those intolerant Christians must be twisting the Bible to support their bigotry."

But, in fact, this conclusion verifies that Jesus was right all along:
The majority of the world's population *will* miss out on heaven. One of
the critics' chief arguments against Christianity actually supports the
veracity of Christ's teachings.

Nevertheless, one wonders how so many people could be so wrong.
From where did all these religions originate? The Bible gives two answers
to that question. First, some of the world's religions are the result of
human invention. Perhaps you've heard the story about the atheist who
went mountain climbing. He was making good progress toward the
summit until his foot slipped and he found himself hanging on to the
fragile branch of a tree. Realizing that the branch could not support him
much longer, he looked up and, out of shear desperation, cried out, "Is
there anybody up there who can help me?"

A voice boomed from the heavens, "Yes, but first you must let go
of the branch."

After a long pause the atheist shouted, "Is there anyone *else* who can
help me?"

It's a funny story that illustrates a serious truth: Those who have
rejected the God of the Bible do so not because of a lack of information

about God, but because of a lack of desire to know the true God on His terms. In Romans 1, the apostle Paul presented the three-step process that explains the development of false religions: (1) Every person on the planet receives a knowledge of the true God through creation, (2) many people reject this knowledge because of their refusal to acknowledge their Creator, and (3) people who have rejected the knowledge of the true God have replaced that knowledge with a god of their own making. As Romans 1:22-23 states, "Professing to be wise, they became fools, and exchanged the glory of the incorruptible God for an image in the form of corruptible man and of birds and four-footed animals and crawling creatures."

If you have ever taken a comparative-religion course in college, you have probably learned about the "evolution of religion." According to this theory, humans began worshiping idols (animism). But as humans evolved, they replaced animism with polytheism (the worship of many gods). Finally, polytheism gave way to monotheism, which is the worship of one God (though different civilizations have different names for that God).

But Robert Brow, an expert in world religions, has demonstrated just the opposite. In his book *Religion: Origins and Ideals,* Brow points out that civilization began with a belief in one God, which was later replaced by the worship of many gods and man-made idols. Why? Did men and women really believe that these new gods—wooden idols, golden statues, cows, and flies—were superior to the one God in whom they had formerly believed? Of course not. As James Montgomery Boice said, they were attracted to these new gods "because they were lesser [gods] and therefore less to be feared."[9] The diversity of religions in the world is not a testimony to humankind's natural godliness, but to our godlessness. We have replaced knowledge of the true God with false gods.

By the way, you see this same kind of "replacement theology" going on today. A few years ago *Christianity Today* published a story about a group of women from mainline denominations who gathered for a so-called reimaging conference where they imagined God as a woman deity named Sophia. The women chanted the following litany to their new god:

> Our maker, Sophia, we are women in your image, with the hot
> blood of our wombs we give form to new life…with our warm
> body fluids we remind the world of its pleasures and sensations.[10]

I will refrain from quoting from the rest of the prayer since women and small children might be reading—but you get the idea. One of the conference attendees said, "I can no longer worship in a theological context that depicts God as an abusive parent and Jesus as the obedient, trusting Child." Another added, "I don't think we need folks hanging on crosses and blood dripping and weird stuff." And still another insightful comment: "If we cannot imagine Jesus as a tree, as a river, as wind, or rain, we are doomed together."[11]

Doomed indeed. "They became futile in their speculations, and their foolish heart was darkened" (Romans 1:21). As someone has said, "God created man in His own image, and ever since that time man has been trying to return the compliment!"

Beyond human invention, the Bible also gives another explanation for the development of false religions: *Satan's deception.* In Psalm 106:36-37, the psalmist explains that those who offer sacrifices to idols are actually sacrificing to demons. In Paul's first letter to Timothy, the apostle reminded the young pastor that in the last days many will follow counterfeit faiths that are really the "doctrines of demons" (4:1). Every time I hear a non-Christian recount a near-death experience in which she sees a bright light at the end of the tunnel and a soothing voice assuring her that she is headed toward heaven, I am reminded of Paul's warning that "Satan disguises himself as an angel of light" (2 Corinthians 11:14). As Jesus said, Satan "is a liar and the father of lies" (John 8:44). Satan's chief deception is to lure people away from the only Source of salvation.

The multitude of false religions—and the accompanying billions of people who follow them—is just more evidence of the truthfulness of Scripture.

4. *"All religions teach basically the same thing."* The crux of this argument goes like this: "No single religion can claim to be the only way to God since they are all teaching the same truth." Only a person who is ignorant of the teachings of the major world religions would make such a statement. Although there may be minor similarities between religions (which can be explained by humankind's desire to retain some of the more pleasant aspects of the truth in whatever religion a person invents), the five major world religions differ significantly on major issues such as salvation and the afterlife. For example, Hinduism worships more than three hundred gods. Hindus identify humankind's chief problem as failing to recognize ourselves as divine beings and thus sentencing ourselves to an endless cycle of birth, death, and rebirth. The only way to break this cycle is through the spiritual development that is achieved through the practice of four yogas.

Buddha, a dissatisfied follower of Hinduism, decided to develop his own name-brand religion built on the premise that humankind's basic problem is the desire for pleasure and status as well as the necessities of life. According to Buddhism, the only way we can ever stop our cravings and enter into the restful state of Nirvana is by following the Noble Eightfold Path.

Islam, which was introduced in the seventh century AD, rejects polytheism and worships Allah ("the God"). Islam removes a lot of the mumbo jumbo about endless cycles of life and death, the four yogas, and Nirvana, and teaches that if you want to go to heaven, you must obey the laws of Allah.

Judaism also claims that obedience to the Law (although a different Law and a different God) is the only path to righteousness.

But in Christianity it is God's actions toward humankind, not humankind's actions toward God, that result in our eternal salvation. As it's been said, "There are not thousands of religions in the world, but only two. All of the other religions of the world are spelled 'd-o.' Regardless of its label, every other religion tells us what we must 'do' to earn God's favor. But Christianity is spelled 'd-o-n-e.' The foundation of the gospel is not what we do for God, but what God has already done for us in sending His Son to atone for our sins."

Let's assume for a moment that there really are only two categories of religion. The first category includes every world religion that claims that salvation, heaven, Nirvana—whatever you want to label it—is achieved by our efforts. The second category says that salvation is an unearnable gift from God. Only Christianity makes that claim. While it is possible that neither category is right, it is impossible that *both* are right. Why? Because both categories are making mutually exclusive claims. Christian apologist Ravi Zacharias writes:

All religions are not the same. All religions do not point to God. All religions *do not say* that all religions are the same. At the heart of *every* religion is an uncompromising commitment to a particular way of defining who God is or is not and accordingly, of defining life's purpose.

Anyone who claims that all religions are the same betrays not only an ignorance of all religions but also a caricatured view of even the best-known ones. Every religion at its core is exclusive.[12]

Philosophically, it is possible that all world religions are wrong, but it is incorrect to assert that they are all basically teaching the same truths.

5. *"It is unfair for God to send people to hell just because they haven't believed in Jesus."* Who would want to serve a God who would sentence people to an eternity of suffering just because they never had an opportunity to hear the gospel? Is it conceivable that the God who determines where people live (Acts 17:26) would condemn those same people to hell just because they lived in a region unreached by the gospel? Such troubling questions led theologian Clark Pinnock to abandon the Bible's emphasis on the "view of judgment which focuses on the much narrower issue of verbal assent to the gospel—or the decision for Christ." He goes on to say,

In particular it contradicts an implication of the thinking that the unevangelized, most of whom have endured oppression and misery in this earthly life, will go on suffering in hell forever because they did not believe in Jesus, even though this is something they could not have done. The implication of popular eschatology is that the downtrodden of this world, unable to call upon Jesus through no fault of their own, are to be rejected for eternity, giving the final victory to the tyrants who trampled them down. Knowing little but suffering in this life, the unevangelized poor will know nothing but more and worse suffering in the next.[13]

To add injury to insult, evangelical Christianity claims that not only are the poor, downtrodden good people who never trust in Christ destined to hell, but those who spend their lives tyrannizing the oppressed yet claim Christ as Savior at the last moment will spend eternity in heaven. Phil Donahue succinctly expresses how ludicrous this seems: "So if a Nazi killed a Jew, a good Jew, practicing Jew, the Jew goes to hell, but the Nazi still has a chance to get to heaven. That would be the consequence of your position."[14]

Admittedly, such a position seems preposterous. So how can we ever assert such a "truth" with a straight face? Are there any rational answers to these five objections to the exclusivity of Christianity?

What to Say to Those Who Object

Let's return for a moment to my in-flight conversation with the "former Christian" who objected to the assertion that Christ is the only way to heaven. Between endless servings of pretzels and Diet Cokes, I attempted to answer the above objections with the following four insights:

1. *"Your argument is with the Bible, not with me."* When Christians claim that faith in Christ is the only way to heaven, they are simply voicing what the Bible teaches. For example, in John 14:6 Jesus said to His apostles, "I am the way, and the truth, and the life; *no one* comes to the Father but through Me."

Or consider the apostle Peter's words to the Jewish religious leaders as he stood trial for healing a sick man in the name of Jesus Christ:

Let it be known to all of you and to all the people of Israel, that by the name of Jesus Christ the Nazarene, whom you crucified, whom God raised from the dead—by this name this man stands here before you in good health.… And there is salvation in *no one* else; for there is *no other* name under heaven that has been given among men by which we must be saved. (Acts 4:10,12)

One more example. In Romans 10 the apostle Paul expressed his deep desire for the salvation of his fellow Israelites (see verses 1-3). Although he commended these Jews for their sincere religious commitment ("zeal for God"), Paul did not believe they possessed the "righteousness of God" (verse 3). How, then, can a God-fearing, law-abiding Jew obtain a right relationship with God? The same way—the only way—anyone else receives it:

If you confess with your mouth Jesus as Lord, and believe in your heart that God raised Him from the dead, you will be saved.… For there is no distinction between Jew and Greek; for the same Lord is Lord of all, abounding in riches for all who call on Him; for "Whoever will call upon the name of the Lord will be saved." (verses 9,12-13)

It is important to emphasize that all three men quoted—Jesus, Peter, and Paul—were *Jews,* not Gentiles. The fallacious but oft-quoted charge that the exclusive claim of Christianity is "anti-Semitic" loses much of its punch when one realizes that the three loudest proponents of the exclusivity of Christianity were devout Jews!

When these verses are cited, skeptics may raise two possible objections. First, skeptics might reply, "Well, that's *your* interpretation of those verses. But other people might interpret them differently." A reply to this is, "Give me just one other logical interpretation of Jesus's words

'No one comes to the Father but through Me' or Peter's words that there is 'salvation in no one else.'"

When asked to provide an alternative interpretation, most people aren't able to offer one. But even if they do, a good question to ask is, "Do you *honestly* believe that is what the verse is saying?" There is always a variety of possible interpretations for anything that is written, whether it be a stop sign, directions on a medicine bottle, or a Scripture passage. But a good (and safe) rule of interpretation is this: "When plain sense makes good sense, seek no other sense."

A second objection skeptics might offer is, "Who are you to say who goes to hell and who doesn't? Shouldn't we leave that decision with God?" It is true, of course, that only God has the right to determine who goes to heaven. But it is also correct to say that God has *already* made that determination, as the Bible states. Christians are simply reporting what God has already decided and revealed in His Word.

Perhaps the following illustration will clarify. Suppose you receive a memo from your employer saying all employees are to report to work the next morning one hour early. Anyone failing to do so will be docked a day's pay. A coworker of yours is home sick the day the memo arrives, so you call him on the phone and say, "I thought you would want to know that you need to be at work tomorrow one hour early or you'll lose a day's salary." Your friend rants and raves about how unfair such an expectation is. "You don't have any right to tell me to come in an hour early. You're not my boss," he argues.

How do you reply to such an outburst? You tell him you are simply reading a memo from the boss. This is not your decision; it is your boss's. You are just relaying the information out of concern for your coworker.

It is crucial to emphasize that the exclusivity of Christianity is not the claim of Christians; it is God's decision. We are simply reading a memo from the Boss. As Franklin Graham writes, "A loyal follower of Jesus does not concoct personal ideas about these matters. All he or she does is faithfully represent the words of the Master."[15]

2. *"Truth by its very nature is exclusive."* As explained in the previous chapter, there is a seismic shift in our culture away from the reality of objective truth toward relative truth. However, that shift is very selective. Everyone accepts the notion of absolute truth at some level. How many possible answers are there to the question, What is the sum of 2 plus 3? or What is the capital of Pennsylvania? Obviously, there is only one correct answer, meaning that every other answer is incorrect. Truth by its nature is exclusive.

Yet a skeptic might counter with the argument that religious truth is not as "exact" as mathematics or geography, mainly because religion deals with the unseen. However, it is always a mistake to assume that something is not real just because it can't be seen.

I will never forget August 2, 1985. In the early hours of that morning, I was landing at Dallas–Fort Worth Airport, preparing to go home and help my wife finish packing for our move later that afternoon to our first pastorate in Eastland, Texas. The pilot awakened me from my slumber with a weather report for the day that included thunderstorms in the late afternoon and early evening. *How inconvenient for a moving day,* I remember thinking to myself. Not as inconvenient as those thunderstorms would be to another group of passengers attempting to land later that day on Delta Flight 191.

As Flight 191's captain, Ted Connors, prepared to land his large jumbo jet at the DFW airport that afternoon, he noticed a strange cloud formation at the end of runway 17L. At first he thought he might go around the cloud. But then he apparently reasoned that he had hundreds of thousands of pounds of aircraft on his side as well as three powerful

Rolls-Royce engines and more than 43,000 hours of experience between his two copilots. Furthermore, other planes ahead of his had just landed on the same runway. How much damage could a little wind and rain cause?

What Captain Connors, a highly competent and cautious pilot, did not realize was that in that cloud were invisible, yet powerful forces at work—wind shear, microbursts, and vortexes. As his plane made its way through the cloud, the forces of nature grabbed the jetliner and threw it against the ground, resulting in the loss of 137 lives.[16]

In an instant the captain apparently made an error in judgment, an error many of us make when dealing with the unseen. We assume that because something is invisible, it is less real and less exact.

But just as there are natural laws of aerodynamics and physics that governed the doomed jetliner, there are spiritual laws that govern our relationship with God. We may think we can alter those laws by approaching a holy God in some other manner than His prescribed Way, but when we do, the result will be spiritual disaster.

3. *"God wants to save as many people as possible, not as few as possible."* Although the exclusivity of Christianity must be affirmed, it is important to note that God loves all people, and His stated desire is to save as many people as possible. Again, let's listen to three of the most vocal proponents of the exclusivity of Christianity and hear what they say about God's desire to save. In 1 Timothy 2:4, the apostle Paul stated that "[God] desires all men to be saved and to come to the knowledge of the truth." The apostle Peter said, "The Lord is not slow about His promise, as some count slowness, but is patient toward you, not wishing for any to perish but for all to come to repentance" (2 Peter 3:9). And Jesus said, "For the Son of Man has come to seek and to save that which was lost" (Luke 19:10).

But someone might ask, "If God really wants to save as many people as possible, what about all those people in the world who have never had the opportunity to hear about Jesus Christ? Is it fair for God to send them to hell just because they have never heard of Him?" That's a fair question, and one that the Bible answers in two ways.

First, the fact that faith in Christ is the only way to be saved should not lead to spiritual smugness. Immediately after explaining that only those who call upon the name of Jesus Christ will be saved, Paul prodded his audience into action with this missionary challenge:

> How then will they call on Him in whom they have not
> believed? How will they believe in Him whom they have
> not heard? And how will they hear without a preacher? How
> will they preach unless they are sent? (Romans 10:14-15)

God has expressed His desired end that as many people as possible be saved. But He has also explained the means by which His desired end is to be accomplished: the worldwide proclamation of the gospel.

Second, the Scriptures teach that God will reveal Himself to those who sincerely want to know Him. As we saw in Romans 1, every person has received a knowledge of the true God through nature. Just by looking into the sky, any person can surmise that there is a powerful Creator-God. As my former seminary professor Dr. Charles Ryrie used to say, "While such knowledge is not enough to save a person, it is enough, if rejected, to condemn a person." Those who have received the knowledge of the true God, rejected it, and then replaced it with a man-made god are without excuse.

However, Scripture strongly suggests that those who respond to that general knowledge of God will be given the special revelation of

Jesus Christ necessary for salvation. For example, consider just three of many biblical illustrations of that principle:

- An Ethiopian court official traveled to Jerusalem to worship the God of Judaism. On his return trip, he was reading from the Old Testament book of Isaiah about the coming Messiah. Confused by the passage, he desperately desired to understand its meaning. So God supernaturally dispatched the evangelist Philip to explain the passage and proclaim the gospel, resulting in the Ethiopian's conversion (see Acts 8:26-40).

- Cornelius, a Roman centurion, worshiped the God of Israel even though he was not a Jew himself. God honored his sincere spiritual quest by sending the apostle Peter to preach the gospel of Jesus Christ to him so that he and his family might be saved (see Acts 10:1-22).

- The apostle Paul "accidentally" encountered disciples of John the Baptist who were living in Ephesus. Although these men were religious, they were also lost. Paul explained the gospel of Christ to them, and they were saved (see Acts 19:1-7).

Notice that in each instance the non-Christians in the story were extremely religious people, yet they were considered lost. In today's culture, Philip, Peter, and Paul (sounds like a singing group, doesn't it?) would be judged as intolerant and inconsiderate for insinuating that the religious beliefs of the Ethiopian official, the Roman centurion, and the disciples of John were somehow inferior to Christianity. But, thankfully, Philip, Peter, and Paul were not slaves of political correctness but were servants of God who courageously spoke the truth. The general knowledge of God these unbelievers possessed was not enough to save them. But their sincere response to their limited understanding motivated God to send them the special knowledge of Christ they needed for salvation.

There is no reason to believe that God doesn't do the same thing today. Are people born into particular countries by accident? Are missionaries assigned to certain people groups around the globe at random? Does an unbeliever looking for answers stumble on to a religious television program in his hotel room by chance? These three examples from the Bible should assure us that those who desire to know God will receive the knowledge they need to trust in Christ. "Light obeyed bringeth more light...but light rejected bringeth night."

4. *"The fact that God has provided one way of salvation demonstrates His love."* While talking with my seatmate on the plane, I decided to save my best argument for the end. (We preacher-types like to build toward a climax whenever possible.) I said to him, "Imagine that this plane we're on crashed." (When the other passengers and the flight attendant gave me dirty looks, I lowered my voice.) "Imagine that this plane crashed, the interior lights went out, and smoke started filling the cabin. The flight attendant stands at the front of the cabin waving her emergency flashlight and saying, 'Follow me. There is one way out.' Would you accuse her of being intolerant for insisting there is only one exit out of the burning jetliner? And if I took your hand and said, 'Follow me,' would you label me a narrow-minded bigot because I was attempting to persuade you to follow me to safety?"

For the first time in several hours, my new friend had no response, so I pressed the illustration a little further. "If indeed there were another exit out of the plane that was closer to you, wouldn't the flight attendant encourage you to use it? The only reason for her dogmatic assertion that there is only one exit available would be because there *is* only one exit available, and she has a sincere desire to lead you to safety."

To be honest, there is one potential flaw with this example. This illustration only makes sense to people who realize that because of their sin, their lives have crashed and they are in danger of facing the fire of God's judgment. Not everyone agrees with that assessment. Malcolm Muggeridge pointed out that human depravity is at once the most empirically verifiable reality and the most philosophically resistant. In spite of the overwhelming evidence on the front pages of the newspaper as well as in the deep recesses of our hearts, many people refuse to accept the notion that we are sinners facing God's judgment. Without the acknowledgment of that bad news, there can be no acceptance of the good news.

Fortunately, my travel companion did not need a preacher to tell him that he had fallen short of God's plan for his life. His past failures and his intuition that there might be a future judgment caused him to listen carefully to my words.

I wish I could end the story by saying that as the plane's wheels touched down and we taxied to the gate, my friend bowed his head and prayed to receive Christ as his Savior. Maybe if I were Billy Graham, that would have happened. Instead, he expressed gratitude for taking the time to talk and said, "You haven't fully convinced me, but I promise you one thing. I'm going to start reading my Bible again and checking out what you said." That was good enough for me.

Obviously no one can be forced to utilize the one escape exit to salvation that God has provided every person. But that should not discourage us from waving the light of the gospel in a dark and sin-filled world so people might discover the only way—God's Way—to eternal life.

God Is Ultimately Responsible
for Suffering

Though a few years have now passed, the date and the horrifying images are indelibly etched in our memories: September 11, 2001. Who will ever forget the sight of two jetliners crashing into the World Trade Center on that crisp, end-of-the-summer morning, while another plane slammed into the Pentagon, and still another suicide mission was aborted in a Pennsylvania field due to the heroic efforts of doomed but determined passengers? Nearly three thousand people lost their lives that day, leaving behind friends and family members who are still trying to cope with the aftermath of such horrific evil.

These kinds of disasters always prompt the inevitable question, If there really is a God, why would He allow such an evil deed to take place? In the months following September 11, there was no shortage of divergent answers to the question, Where was God on September 11? For example, Lisa Beamer, wife of Todd Beamer who led the charge to thwart the terrorists on United Flight 93, believes her husband was on that plane by divine appointment and that the tragedy served a higher purpose known only to God.[1]

However, the mother of another passenger on that doomed flight refuses to believe that God or fate played any part in the tragedy. "It's easier to think it was fate," said Joan Glick, mother of Jeremy Glick.

"Then everyone is off the hook, the government, the airlines, the security people. If people start to believe it was fate, that means there is no way you could have controlled the destiny of September 11."[2]

Cheryl McGuiness, wife of American Airlines pilot Tom McGuiness whose plane slammed into the first World Trade Center building, does not believe that God caused the hijackers to crash those planes into the World Trade Center. Nevertheless, when she spoke to our congregation some months later, she expressed her confidence that God could turn such tragedy into a blessing for her and her family.

One popular religious writer expressed still another viewpoint. "Where was God on September 11? God was with the firemen, policemen, and rescue workers searching for survivors. And he was with the grieving families, weeping alongside them." When asked why God did not prevent the tragedy, the writer explained that God would have liked to stop the evil, but He has restricted Himself from supernaturally intervening in human affairs.

Two other well-known religious figures offered the highly unpopular opinion that this tragedy was the result of God's judgment on America for such sins as homosexuality and abortion. Understandably, that viewpoint was roundly condemned not only by the secular media but by other religionists, prompting one of the ministers to retract his statement and the other to claim that his comments had been taken "out of context."

Terrorist attacks, child murders, and worldwide starvation, as well as personal tragedies in our individual worlds naturally cause us to wonder about God's role in human suffering. Author and theologian John Stott states, "The fact of suffering undoubtedly constitutes the single greatest challenge to the Christian faith."[3]

Stott's assertion is not a simple case of religious hyperbole. For his book *The Case for Faith*, Lee Strobel commissioned a survey of a cross section of American adults, asking this question: "If you could ask God only one question, and you knew He would give you an answer, what would you ask?" The top response? "Why is there pain and suffering in the world?"[4]

ONE QUESTION—FOUR POSSIBLE ANSWERS

Throughout the ages, many have used this question in an effort to discredit the Christian faith, and they continue that same assault today. Eighteenth-century Scottish philosopher David Hume tried to "impale Christian theology upon one or both horns of his famous dilemma: 'Is [God] willing to prevent evil, but not able? Then he is impotent. Is he able, but not willing? Then he is malevolent. Is he both able and willing? Whence then is evil?'"[5] Hume offered two possible explanations for evil that go something like this:

1. If God is gracious and loving and still allows evil, it is because He is unable to prevent it.
2. If God is able to prevent suffering, but doesn't, it is because He is evil.

If you refuse to accept either of the above alternatives, you must agree with Hume's implied third conclusion: There is no God, since evil runs rampant in our world.

In reality, there is a fourth explanation for evil that Hume understandably omitted. But before we discuss that option, let's look at these three possible explanations for God's role in suffering in the world, starting with Hume's implied conclusion denying the existence of God.

"There Is No God"

This morning's newspaper carried the heartbreaking story of a fourteen-year-old-girl from the western United States who was kidnapped by a next-door neighbor, then dismembered and decapitated. If there really is a good and loving God as portrayed in the Bible, surely He would not allow such a horrendous act. The fact that such atrocities do occur on a regular (and seemingly increasing) basis is the smoking gun proving that no such God exists...or so the argument goes.

But as Bob and Gretchen Passantino point out, by employing this line of reasoning "the skeptic assumes parts of the Christian world view in order to indict the Christian God, but he is unwilling to acknowledge the other parts of the Christian world view that answer his indictments."[6] Let me explain.

By using the existence of evil to disprove the existence of God, the skeptic is assuming that there is such a thing as evil. But apart from a belief in God, can anything really be termed "evil"? What makes decapitating a teenage girl evil? "Well, it's against the law," the skeptic answers. But are man-made laws always reliable means to distinguish between good and evil?

In our nation's history, there was a time when the law permitted slavery, but did that make slavery right? Other cultures allow children to be sacrificed to pagan deities, but is that morally permissible just because the law allows it? Surely we are not going to assume that human laws are an infallible guide for defining good and evil.

It is impossible to have any consistent basis for defining evil without the existence of an absolute moral law. And it is impossible to have an absolute moral law without a moral Creator who stamps every human heart made in His image with a sense of right and wrong.

"But couldn't our sense of right and wrong come from our evolutionary development, rather than from a Divine Creator?" Apologist Ravi Zacharias explains how illogical it is to look to evolution to explain our innate sense of good and evil:

This attempt to deny God because of the presence of evil is so fraught with the illogical that one marvels at its acceptance. Not one proponent of evolutionary ethics has explained how an impersonal, amoral first cause through a nonmoral process has produced a moral basis of life, while at the same time denying any objective moral basis for good and evil. Does it not seem odd that of all the permutations and combinations that a random universe might afford we should end up with the notions of the true, the good, and the beautiful? In reality, why call anything good or evil? Why not call it orange or purple?[7]

Translation: If we are nothing but the random fusing together of cells, how can we explain our deep sense of right and wrong? If, as atheist Richard Dawkins claims, the universe is indifferent to what we call evil and good and cares about neither, then why do *we* care about both?

The presence of evil in the world, and our awareness of that evil, argues strongly for, not against, a Divine Creator.

"God Is Evil"

Frankly, you don't hear too many people articulating this possibility, although theoretically it could be true were it not for the revelation of Scripture. Yet, even though it is unpopular to publicly refer to God as a tyrant, some people privately harbor this feeling about their Creator and turn away from Him. Media mogul Ted Turner, who once labeled Christianity as "a religion for losers," did not always feel that way. When he was younger, Turner attended a Christian prep school. He says that during that period of time, "I think I was saved seven or eight times." But one event dramatically altered his feelings toward God. His younger sister became very ill, and Turner prayed for five years that God would heal her. When she died, Turner became disillusioned and had no further use for a God who would allow that kind of suffering. "I began to lose my faith," he said, "and the more I lost it the better I felt."[8]

"God Would Like to Help, But He Can't"

Since no one wants to think of his or her Creator as evil, this possibility seems to offer a more palatable and logical answer to suffering in the world. "God loves us deeply and truly grieves when His creatures grieve. However, God is limited in His ability to intervene in human affairs." What is it that limits God's ability to prevent suffering? you may wonder.

Some argue that God is limited by *His own nature*. Rabbi Harold Kushner, after watching his young son die of progeria—a rare disease causing premature and rapid aging—came to the conclusion that "even God has hard time keeping chaos in check" and that God is a "God of justice and not of power."[9] Kushner concludes his best-selling book *When Bad Things Happen to Good People* with these words:

> Are you capable of forgiving and loving God even when you
> have found out that He is not perfect, even when He has let you
> down and disappointed you by permitting bad luck and sickness
> and cruelty in His world, and permitting some of those things
> to happen to you? Can you learn to love and forgive Him
> despite His limitations, as Job does, and as you once learned to
> forgive and love your parents even though they were not as wise,
> as strong, or as perfect as you needed them to be?[10]

With a few strokes of the pen, Kushner has reduced God to an imperfect, limited, and less-than-all-wise-and-all-powerful monarch.

Responding to Kushner's assertion, another Jewish writer said, "If that's who God is, why doesn't he resign and let someone more competent take his place?"[11]

Others say that God is unable to stop evil because of *natural laws* He has put into place. Every accident, earthquake, famine, or illness is the result of inviolate laws of nature that God cannot suspend, no matter how much He would like to. In other words, God has voluntarily handcuffed Himself and thrown away the key.

Yet those who propose such an explanation for God's nonintervention tend to be inconsistent. For example, Dr. Erwin Lutzer tells the true story about a group of ministers who met together for a prayer breakfast after one of California's earthquakes a few years ago. The shifting freeways and destroyed buildings were the result of natural phenomena, not a divine plan, they agreed. Earthquakes are to be expected in a fallen world, and God has nothing to do with them. Yet when one of the ministers closed the meeting in prayer, he thanked God for timing the earthquake at five o'clock in the morning when few cars were on the highway. When he concluded the prayer, the rest of the ministers added a heartfelt "Amen."[12]

Although God could not control the earthquake's occurrence, for some reason the ministers felt that He could control its timing. But beyond such inconsistencies in logic, there looms a larger question: If God has become captive to His own natural laws and is incapable of intervening, then why bother to pray?

Thankfully, the Bible reminds us that natural forces do not hold our supernatural God hostage. One can only imagine how many laws of physics and biology were violated by the parting of the Red Sea, the virgin birth of Christ, the feeding of the five thousand, and the resurrection of Christ from the dead.

Finally, some say that God's inability to prevent suffering is due to *humankind's free will*. Although God wishes the killer would not decapitate the teenage girl, God is powerless to stop him because to do so would mean tampering with the most sacred of divine gifts: freedom.

Since the Garden of Eden, God has imbued humankind with the ability and responsibility to choose between good and evil. Unfortunately, many choose the latter, and we must all suffer the consequences of those poor choices. Again, people embrace this viewpoint selectively rather than consistently. For example, consider Rabbi Kushner's answer to the question that naturally arises from his theology of a God who is incapable of intervening in our daily affairs:

> How does God make a difference in our lives if He neither kills nor cures? God inspires people to help other people who have been hurt by life, and by helping them, they protect them from the danger of feeling alone, abandoned, or judged. God makes some people want to become doctors and nurses, to spend days and nights of self-sacrificing concern with an intensity for which no money can compensate.... God moves people to want to be medical researchers, to focus their intelligence and energy on the causes and possible cures for some of life's tragedies.[13]

Do you see the gross inconsistency here? God cannot stop one person from assaulting another because that would be a violation of human freedom, but He can cause another person to choose to be a doctor so that he can help the victim of a random assault! God cannot prevent someone from contracting cancer, but He can override a person's vocational choice and lead her to become an oncologist to care for the cancer victim. You can't have it both ways! Either God is in control or He isn't.

By the way, the idea of a God who is unwilling or unable to override natural laws or human freedom is not limited to Jewish rabbis. Some Christian theologians are now embracing a flavor of this view through "open theism." According to this perspective, God's knowledge of the future is limited to what *He* will do, not what humans will do. Thus, God is in the position of constantly waiting upon and reacting to His creatures. John Sanders, a leading proponent of open theism, writes,

> God has chosen not to control every detail that happens in our lives. Moreover, God has flexible strategies. Though the divine nature does not change, God reacts to contingencies, even adjusting his plans, if necessary, to take into account the decisions of his free creatures. God is endlessly resourceful and wise in working toward the fulfillment of his ultimate goals.... God's plan is not a detailed script or blueprint, but a broad intention that allows for a variety of options regarding precisely how his goals may be reached.[14]

If Sanders were rewriting the opening words of *The Four Spiritual Laws* evangelistic tract, he might begin with "God loves you and has a wonderful plan for your life. But if that plan doesn't work, He has Plan B. And if you or someone else messes up that plan, there is always Plan C or D."

In the next section we will discover what the Bible says about the extent of God's control over all of His creation, whether it be humankind, the laws of nature, or even Satan himself. But I think it is worth pointing out that personal tragedies led both Sanders and Kushner (and I suspect many others) to conclude that God must not be in complete control of His creation. Sanders explains, "When I was in high school one of my brothers was killed in a motorcycle accident. For the first time, I began to think about God's role in human affairs—was God responsible for my brother's death?"[15]

John Sanders and Harold Kushner believe that there is a God and that He is loving, not sadistic. Therefore, how can they possibly reconcile a loving God with human misery without concluding that God must be limited in His ability to alleviate suffering and evil?

Obviously, there is another alternative: God exists, He is loving and all-powerful, *and* He assumes full responsibility for everything that happens in His creation. Such an idea is not only grounded in Scripture, but it is also the only answer that provides genuine and lasting comfort to those who find themselves caught in the maelstrom of inexplicable heartache and unanswered questions.

THE GOD OF THE BIBLE

In his book *The Knowledge of the Holy,* A. W. Tozer wrote, "What comes to our minds when we think about God is the most important thing about us."[16] Unfortunately, many people believe in a God of their imaginations rather than the God revealed in Scripture. The idolatry that was so roundly condemned in the Old Testament was reducing God and His majesty to a deity of our own making. People like Kushner and Sanders (as well as you and me) do the same thing today by discarding those attributes of God that we find distasteful and retaining those characteristics that are more appealing. Dorothy Sayers has written that we have "very efficiently pared the claws of the Lion of Judah...and recommended him as a fitting household pet for...pious old ladies."[17]

What does the Bible reveal about the true God and His relationship to suffering and evil? I'd better warn you that some of the following statements may cause you to wince a little or even to slam this book shut in disgust. But before you do, give me until the end of the chapter to demonstrate why we can enthusiastically embrace the politically incorrect belief that God is ultimately responsible for all suffering.

God Is in Control of All His Creation

The psalmist declared that "The LORD has established His throne in the heavens, and His sovereignty rules over all" (Psalm 103:19). This verse gives us a perfect definition of *sovereignty:* to rule over *everything.* A ruler cannot be semisovereign anymore than a woman can be semipregnant. Either He is in control or He is not. The Bible affirms God's rule over *all* of humankind, over *all* of His created beings (including Satan), and over *all* circumstances:

But our God is in the heavens;
He does *whatever He pleases.* (Psalm 115:3)

I know that you can do *anything* and that *no one* can stop you. (Job 42:2, TLB)

All the inhabitants of the earth are accounted as nothing,
But He does according to His will in the host of heaven
And among the inhabitants of earth;
And *no one* can ward off His hand
Or say to Him, "What have You done?" (Daniel 4:35)

We have obtained an inheritance, having been predestined according to His purpose who works *all things* after the counsel of His will. (Ephesians 1:11)

Nowhere does the Bible teach, as Sanders implies, that God has a Plan A and a Plan B depending on the choices we humans make. God has one plan that governs all of His creation. It is a plan that was formulated before the creation of the universe and was broad enough to include Lucifer's rebellion against God, Adam and Eve's sin in the garden, the slaughter of thousands of Hebrew babies in Egypt, and even the crucifixion of God's own Son.

If you think about it for a moment, you can understand how illogical it is to believe in the kind of semisovereign God who, as John Sanders writes, has chosen "not to control every detail that happens in our lives." For example, Psalm 139 clearly teaches that God carefully planned every part of our bodies before we were born:

> For You formed my inward parts;
> You wove me in my mother's womb.
> I will give thanks to You, for I am fearfully and wonderfully
>   made. (verses 13-14)

Think of the extraordinary events God had to orchestrate to arrange for your father and mother to meet one another, fall in love, and marry so that their unique DNA would combine to form you. Obviously, God's control had to extend beyond the union of your parents to include your grandparents, great-grandparents, and on and on. Steve Farrar explains that God's micromanagement of our genetics had to include every sperm and egg in our family chain all the way back to Adam: "If God had missed even one of those tiny details, you wouldn't exist. But God never misses anything, and He's seen to it that you do exist. You are not here by accident."[18]

But as political writer William Safire points out, "The candidate who takes credit for the rain gets blamed for the drought." If God is going to claim control over all His creation, then He must also assume responsibility for the evil that is in the world. Amazingly, He does just that. For example, God unabashedly assumes responsibility for physical suffering: "Who has made man's mouth? Or who makes him mute or deaf, or seeing or blind? Is it not I, the LORD?" (Exodus 4:11).

In today's religious culture it is more politically correct to assign the blame for handicapped children to random mutations, irresponsible doctors, negligent parents, the effects of living in a fallen world, or even to Satan himself. But God says, "No, I'm the One responsible. If you are looking for someone to blame, start with Me."

What about wars, famines, or tragedies like September 11? If God is completely in control, then He must be responsible for those events as well. Again, He assures us that He is:

I am the LORD, and there is no other,

The One forming light and creating darkness,

Causing well-being and *creating calamity;*

I am the LORD who does all these. (Isaiah 45:6-7)

Some theologians, in their attempt to let God off the hook for tragedies in the world, make the distinction between God's *causing* and God's *allowing* suffering. They cite the travails of the Old Testament patriarch Job and point out that it was Satan, not God, who tormented this man of faith. God's role was reduced to simply allowing Satan to rob Job of his wealth, his children, and his health.

But if God is not the direct cause of suffering and yet He has the power to prevent it, isn't He at the very least guilty of negligence? For example, if you see an elderly woman being assaulted on the street, and you have the power to stop the attacker but fail to do so, aren't you in some way culpable? To allow suffering when you are capable of preventing suffering is to be responsible for suffering.

God Is Good, Not Evil

Perhaps you have not found a lot a comfort in the verses cited above. Taken by themselves, they only reveal that God is responsible for all the evil in His universe. But is God's sovereignty alone enough to comfort us in our affliction?

I once listened to a television interview with the former mistress of an infamous Middle Eastern dictator. She explained that for entertainment the dictator watched videos of prisoners being tortured. (I guess they don't have a Blockbuster in his country.) How do we know that God is not a sadistic sovereign, delighting in the pain He inflicts on His subjects? The Bible assures us that our sovereign God is also a good and loving God:

> The LORD is compassionate and gracious,
> Slow to anger and abounding in *lovingkindness.* (Psalm 103:8)

> Oh give thanks to the LORD, for He is *good;*
> For His *lovingkindness* is everlasting. (Psalm 107:1)

> This is the message we have heard from Him and announce to you, that God is Light, and in Him there is *no darkness* at all. (1 John 1:5)

> The one who does not love does not know God, for God is *love.* (1 John 4:8)

Pastor and author Max Lucado explains the practical implication of this theological reality of God's love:

> Probe deep within him. Explore every corner. Search every angle. Love is all you find. Go to the beginning of every decision he has made and you'll find it. Go to the end of every story he has told and you'll see it.
>
> Love.
>
> No bitterness. No evil. No cruelty. Just love. Flawless love. Passionate love. Vast and pure love. He is love....
>
> The same God who was mighty enough to carve out the canyon is tender enough to put hair on the legs of the Matterhorn Fly to keep it warm. The same force that provides symmetry to the planets guides the baby kangaroo to its mother's pouch before the mother knows it is born.[19]

Yet, as consoling as those declarations of God's love are, how do we reconcile God's love with the horrendous evil we see in the world?

Much of the Suffering in the World Is Self-Inflicted

The British writer G. K. Chesterton once sent the following letter to the editor of a newspaper: "Dear Sir: In response to your article 'What's Wrong with the World'—I AM. Faithfully yours, G. K. Chesterton." Indeed, much of the misery in the world as well as in our own lives is a direct result of what we do to others or what we do to ourselves. The brutal crimes described in the newspapers, the emotional suffering and financial hardships that so often accompany divorce, or the illnesses that result from poor lifestyle habits can hardly be blamed on God. Instead, they are the results of our wrong choices or the wrong choices of others.

As Philip Yancey says in *Where Is God When It Hurts?* "The Bible traces the entrance of suffering and evil into the world to a grand but terrible quality of human beings—freedom." Suffering is the price we continue paying for the freedom to choose between right and wrong.

Sometimes our wrong choices result in God's direct judgment against us. For example, God warned the Israelites: "If you do not obey the LORD your God, to observe to do all His commandments and His statutes with which I charge you today, that all these curses will come upon you and overtake you" (Deuteronomy 28:15). God then lists every kind of judgment imaginable—from devastating famines to incurable fevers—that would be attributable to the violation of His commands.

The link between humankind's sin and God's judgment is not limited to the Israelites. Scripture teaches that Christians who flaunt God's laws can also expect God's judgment: "For those whom the Lord loves He disciplines, and He scourges every son whom He receives" (Hebrews 12:6).

God's refusal to allow us to disobey Him without severe consequences is proof that we are part of His family. However, the fact that God's discipline toward His children is motivated by love doesn't eliminate the pain. As author Jamie Buckingham said, "He whom God loveth, He beateth the hell out of."

I realize it is unpopular in today's culture to link suffering with sin. People are quick to cite the experience of Job as evidence that suffering is not always attributable to sin. We discover in the first two chapters of Job's story that the loss of his family, his wealth, and his health had nothing to with his poor choices or his deliberate rebellion against his Creator. In fact, the writer describes Job in the opening words of the story as "blameless, upright, fearing God, and turning away from evil" (Job 1:1).

Yet, it would be a mistake to extrapolate from Job's experience that suffering is *never* the result of sin. The Bible seems to indicate that much, if not most, of the adversity that enters our lives can be traced to our own disobedience or to the disobedience of others. When we honestly evaluate the darkness in our own hearts, as C. S. Lewis notes, the question changes from "Why do we suffer?" to "Why don't we suffer *more?*"

Nevertheless, the fact that some of the evil that invades our lives is not directly attributable to sin causes us to wonder why a sovereign and loving God would allow it.

God Uses Short-Term Suffering to Accomplish Long-Term Good

There is a famous analogy that is often used to illustrate that suffering and evil are a matter of perspective. Imagine a hunter stumbling upon a bear caught in a trap. Feeling compassion for the animal, the hunter wants to free the bear. The bear, not understanding the hunter's good intentions, refuses to allow the hunter near him. But the hunter refuses to give up. He shoots the bear with darts full of drugs. Yet the bear still doesn't understand and is convinced that the hunter is trying to kill him.

While the bear is drugged, the hunter has to push the bear further into the trap in order to release the tension on the spring and remove his leg. The bear, in a semiconscious state, now has even more evidence that the hunter is trying to inflict as much pain as possible. But the bear is wrong. He has reached his conclusion prematurely. If he will suspend judgment a little longer, he will see that the hunter was really working on his behalf.[20]

One writer has said that God will always seem unfair to a person trapped in time. Because of our limited perspective and our propensity toward premature judgments, we often arrive at the wrong conclusion regarding God's goodness and wisdom. Every dart of adversity that stings us and every push from the Hunter that plunges us further into the jaws of suffering convince us that God must be up to no good. Yet Scripture reveals three insights about God's plan for our lives that give us a different perspective about suffering:

1. God's purpose for our lives is good. The Bible assures us that "God causes all things to work together for good to those who love [Him], to those who are called according to His purpose" (Romans 8:28). Unfortunately, we often define "good" in terms of a full bank account, a satisfying marriage, an illness-free existence, or a disaster-proof life. But Paul quickly explains in the next verse the good for which God is working all things in our lives: "For those whom He foreknew, He also predestined to become conformed to the image of His Son, so that He would be the firstborn among many brethren" (Romans 8:29).

God's major purpose—His only purpose—in your life is to reshape your attitudes, actions, and affections to perfectly mirror those of His Son, Jesus Christ.

2. God's purpose for our lives requires discomfort. Such a massive renovation project in our lives obviously requires some serious "hammering," resulting in temporary, but nevertheless real, pain. C. S. Lewis used this analogy:

Imagine yourself as a living house. God comes in to rebuild that house. At first, perhaps, you can understand what He is doing. He is getting the drains right and stopping the leaks in the roof and so on…. But presently He starts knocking the house about in a way that hurts abominably and does not seem to make sense. What on earth is He up to? The explanation is that He is building quite a different house from the one you thought of—

throwing out a new wing here, putting on an extra floor there, running up towers, making courtyards. You thought you were going to be made into a decent little cottage: but He is building a palace. He intends to come and live in it Himself.[21]

If you have ever been involved in a major renovation project (as our family is as I write these words), you know there are many times when you find it difficult to visualize the end result, you wonder if the work will ever end, and you question your sanity for ever beginning such an effort in the first place. The most discouraging phase of the project is at midpoint when the familiar has been ripped out but has not yet been replaced with the new, which leads to a third insight.

3. *God's purpose for our lives will be ultimately realized.* One day, at long last, that renovation project is completed, and you deem the final product well worth the temporary inconveniences. God's Word assures us that only at the end of time when Christ returns—and not one moment before—we will finally be able to fully grasp God's purpose for the pain He has brought into our lives.

Not long ago I conducted a funeral service at a church where I had formerly served. Also attending the service were a number of former staff members whom I hadn't seen for many years. After the funeral we stood on the sidewalk outside the sanctuary and reminisced about some of the hard experiences we had all shared at the church. As we told story after story, we laughed so hard we cried. Yet twenty years earlier when we were actually going through those experiences, no one was laughing. What made the difference? Perspective. Looking back, we were able to see how God had used those hard circumstances to prepare us for greater and more satisfying places of ministry.

Trying to be happy when facing a serious illness, dealing with a rebellious child, or standing over the open grave of the person who meant everything to you is impossible. Such an unrealistic expectation placed on us by well-meaning but extremely naive people only adds to our heartache. But one day, the Bible promises, from the vantage point of eternity, Christians will be able to look back, and we will smile as we see how God turned tragedy into triumph:

> Beloved, do not be surprised at the fiery ordeal among you, which comes upon you for your testing, as though some strange thing were happening to you; but to the degree that you share the sufferings of Christ, keep on rejoicing, *so that also at the revelation of His glory* you may rejoice with exultation. (1 Peter 4:12-13)

On that day Christ's followers will stand together on the other side of the grave, and we will laugh until we cry.

Suffering Is Often Beyond Comprehension

But until that time we must resist the urge to offer pat answers or simplistic explanations to those who find themselves in a maelstrom of sorrow. We all remember Job's friends who concluded (wrongly) that Job's suffering was caused by his sin. God silenced those friends by saying, "You have not spoken of Me what is right as My servant Job has" (Job 42:7). If I were God, I would have continued, "Now let Me explain to you why Job suffered. Last April Satan came to Me and said, 'The only reason Job serves You is because You are good to him. But if You let me attack him, then he won't serve You.' So we engaged in this little wager and…"

Interestingly, God never explained to either Job's friends or to Job himself the real reason for the catastrophes that battered Job. Instead, the gist of God's speeches to Job was, "Trust Me. I know what I'm doing."

Similarly, when Jesus was questioned about evils in the world, such as a man's blindness since birth, the slaughter of innocent worshipers, or the collapse of a tower, He never attempted to answer the "Why?" question. Why? Not because there is no answer, but because the answer is beyond comprehension for those of us who are trapped in time.

If we can't offer a complete explanation for suffering, what reassuring words can we offer those who are victims of evil?

First, God is in control of every circumstance in our lives. When people want to challenge the assertion that God assumes responsibility for suffering and evil in the world, they will usually cite the most horrific cases imaginable: the torture of children, the genocide of entire races, and the starvation of millions around the globe. I always respond by directing them to Peter's explanation at Pentecost for the death of Jesus Christ: "This Man, delivered over by the predetermined plan and foreknowledge of God, you nailed to a cross by the hands of godless men and put Him to death" (Acts 2:23).

Who was responsible for the crucifixion of Christ? It was godless men who nailed Him to the cross and who will be judged for their rejection of the Son of God. Nevertheless, their actions were part of the "predetermined plan and foreknowledge of God." Interestingly, a few chapters later the disciples went a step further and claimed that their rejection of Christ was not only *known* by God, it was actually *planned* by God:

> For truly in this city there were gathered together against Your holy servant Jesus, whom You anointed, both Herod and Pontius Pilate, along with the Gentiles and the peoples of Israel, to do whatever Your hand and Your purpose predestined to occur.
> (Acts 4:27-28)

The relationship between God's sovereignty and human responsibility is a mystery that can never be comprehended this side of heaven. Nevertheless, don't miss the point. If God is willing to assume full responsibility for the greatest injustice of all time—the crucifixion of His own Son—He is willing to take responsibility for any evil you and I experience.

Second, God understands our suffering. The fact that Jesus Christ took on human form means that He has endured the same pain you and I experience. He knows what it feels like to be betrayed by family and friends or to stand over the grave of a loved one and weep uncontrollably. He even knows what it is like to feel alienated from God. As Jesus slowly suffocated to death on the cross, He gasped, "My God, My God, why have You forsaken Me?" (Matthew 27:46). Even though God has orchestrated the suffering in our lives for a great eternal purpose and knows the positive outcome of our suffering, He still weeps when we weep.

Author Bryan Chapell says that he has watched the movie *It's a Wonderful Life* dozens of time and knows that, in the end, everything turns out fine for the main character, George Bailey. He knows that his friends and family will rally around him and that Clarence the angel will get his wings. Yet knowing the outcome does not prevent Bryan from experiencing the distress and tears of seeing the pharmacist boxing young George's ears or the pain of seeing what would have happened to Mr. Martini if George hadn't been born. Bryan says it hurts to hear Donna Reed tell Jimmy Stewart to leave the house, even though he knows that they will be reunited in the end. Knowing the outcome does not remove the hurt.[22]

Similarly, although God knows the eventual result of our suffering—because He planned the result—He still weeps with us. In describing the ministry of Jesus Christ on our behalf, the writer of Hebrews assures us that "we do not have a high priest who cannot sympathize with our weaknesses, but One who has been tempted in all things as we are, yet without sin" (Hebrews 4:15). In some mysterious way, the same God who planned the horror of the Crucifixion also felt the pain of the Crucifixion. And because of that He feels our pain as well.

Finally, God has not yet revealed *the final chapter in my story.* (But it has been *written* since the foundation of the world.) Had the curtain closed on that Friday afternoon when Jesus said, "It is finished," then the Crucifixion would have been a real travesty. In spite of thirty-three years of believing in the goodness and wisdom of God, Jesus would have concluded His life doubting that goodness and wisdom. "My God, My God, why have You forsaken Me" would have been His final thought about His heavenly Father.

But, of course, the story didn't end there. When God reached down into the tomb and released His Son from the jaws of death on that Easter Sunday, suddenly all the world understood what the Hunter was doing. Tragedy was suddenly turned to triumph. Only from the vantage point of an empty tomb are we now able to label "good" what seemed so evil just a few days earlier.

I know some who are reading this are experiencing the same kinds of doubts and disappointment that Jesus Christ felt on that Friday afternoon. You wonder why God would allow your mate to desert you, a friend to betray you, your family member to be taken from you, or that illness to strike you. Remember, the story is not complete. The final chapter has not been revealed. As author Tony Campolo says, "It's Friday, but Sunday's comin'!"

God Sends Good People to Hell

The pit is prepared, the fire is made ready, the furnace is now hot, ready to receive them; the flames do now rage and glow. The glittering sword is whet, and held over them, and the pit has opened its mouth under them.... O sinner! Consider the fearful danger you are in."[1] So warned Puritan preacher Jonathan Edwards in his classic sermon "Sinners in the Hands of an Angry God." Though Edwards simply read the message from a sermon manuscript, sans the sweat and bombast that would accompany evangelists in later years, his colorful description of hell sent his audience into convulsions of weeping and repentance. Today, such a message would send many congregants out the door looking for a new more "seeker-sensitive" church.

The idea of God's dispatching people to a place of eternal torment simply because they have not believed the right doctrinal truths has always been repulsive to many. Colonel Robert Ingersoll, a famous atheist of the nineteenth century, railed against the concept of hell: "The idea of hell was born of revenge and brutality on one side, and cowardice on the other.... I have no respect for any human being who believes in it.... I dislike the doctrine, I hate it, I despise it, I defy this doctrine.... This doctrine of hell is infamous beyond all power to express."[2] The renowned philosopher Bertrand Russell rejected not only the Christian religion but the founder of the religion, Jesus Christ, mainly because of His teaching about hell:

There is one very serious defect to my mind in Christ's moral character, and that is that He believed in hell. I do not myself feel that any person who is really profoundly humane can believe in everlasting punishment.[3]

How's that for hubris? "Jesus was a pretty good person except for this one fatal flaw in His character: He chose to believe in hell, and therefore, He is not as moral as I am."

But unbelievers are not the only ones who find the idea of an eternal place of torment politically incorrect. A 1981 survey revealed that only 50 percent of theology faculty believe that hell exists.[4] Nearly half of all seminary students believe that it is in "poor taste" to tell unbelievers that hell is their destination if they reject Christ, and only one in ten evangelical college and seminary students said that warning unbelievers about hell should be the first step in evangelism.[5] While nearly 60 percent of Americans believe in some kind of hell, only 4 percent believe that *they* are going there.[6]

Furthermore, both theologians and laypeople are increasingly revising their beliefs about hell. For example, a few years ago Pope John Paul II announced that hell "is not a punishment imposed externally by God" but is instead a person's own choice to be separated from God, and that "the thought of hell...must not create anxiety or despair, but is a necessary and healthy reminder of freedom."[7] Indeed, more and more theologians are emphasizing hell as a place characterized by an absence of God rather than by the presence of real and painful suffering. Why? Professor Douglas Groothuis of Denver Seminary explains that many Christians today are ashamed of hell and see it as "a blemish to be covered up by the cosmetic of divine love."[8] Jeffrey Sheler, writing in *U.S. News and World Report*, summarizes the result of this rethinking of hell: "[Jonathan] Edwards would scarcely recognize the hell of today. After decades of near obscurity, the netherworld has taken on a new image: more of a deep funk than a pit of fire…suggesting that hell may not be so hot after all."[9]

Whether we eradicate the idea of hell altogether or simply attempt to renovate it by turning down the temperature a bit, are we correct in doing so? As I mentioned earlier, atheist Robert Ingersoll rejected the idea of a place of eternal torment. On one occasion after Ingersoll had delivered a "hot" lecture on the absurdity of hell and assured his audience that every respected intellectual had dismissed the idea of hell, a drunk approached him and said, "Bob, I liked your lecture; I liked what you said about hell. But, Bob, I want you to be sure about it, because I'm depending on you."[10]

Are we safe in allowing people like Russell and Ingersoll to shape our beliefs about hell? Or is there Someone more qualified to tell us what really happens to those who reject the gospel?

JESUS ON HELL

One has to at least credit Bertrand Russell for his intellectual honesty in realizing that rejecting hell requires rejecting Jesus Christ Himself. Thirteen percent of the 1,850 verses in the New Testament that record the words of Jesus deal with the subject of eternal judgment and hell. In fact, Jesus had more to say about hell than He did about heaven. Given Jesus's extensive teaching about hell, it is contradictory to say, "I accept Jesus as a great moral teacher or even as the Son of God, but I refuse to accept His teaching about hell." If Jesus were wrong about hell, it is because (1) He was sincerely mistaken, which disqualifies Him from being the Son of God because He really does not know what awaits people on the other side of the grave, or (2) He was deceptive, which also disqualifies Him from being either the Son of God or even a nice person because He intentionally misled people. But if you accept Jesus Christ as the Son of God, then it is impossible to dismiss what He revealed to us concerning the fate of unbelievers.

What did Jesus have to say about hell? Perhaps Jesus's most vivid description of hell is found in a story He told about two men who lived very different lives—and experienced two different destinies:

> Now there was a rich man, and he habitually dressed in purple and fine linen, joyously living in splendor every day. And a poor man named Lazarus was laid at his gate, covered with sores, and longing to be fed with the crumbs which were falling from the rich man's table; besides, even the dogs were coming and licking his sores.
>
> Now the poor man died and was carried away by the angels to Abraham's bosom; and the rich man also died and was buried. In Hades he lifted up his eyes, being in torment, and saw Abraham far away and Lazarus in his bosom. And he cried out and said, "Father Abraham, have mercy on me, and send Lazarus, so that he may dip the tip of his finger in water and cool off my tongue, for I am in agony in this flame."
>
> But Abraham said, "Child, remember that during your life you received your good things, and likewise Lazarus bad things; but now he is being comforted here, and you are in agony. And besides all this, between us and you there is a great chasm fixed, so that those who wish to come over from here to you will not be able, and that none may cross over from there to us." (Luke 16:19-26)

Many believe that since Jesus used a real name, Lazarus—which means "God is my Helper"—this is probably a true story rather than a parable. Either way, Jesus revealed three important truths about hell.

First, Jesus taught that hell is an actual place. In the New Testament one finds three different Greek words that are all translated "hell" in most English versions of the Bible. The word *tartaros* is used only in 2 Peter 2:4 to describe the place where a special class of wicked angels have been sent because of a sin described in Jude 6.

The most commonly used word for hell is *Gehenna,* used by Jesus eleven times to describe the eternal destiny of those who reject Christ. The word *Gehenna* refers to the Valley of Hinnon, which was located south of Jerusalem. During the reigns of the wicked kings Ahaz and Manasseh, some Israelites offered their children as burnt offerings to the false god Molech. Later the valley was used as a garbage dump where both refuse and the bodies of executed criminals were burned. One can hardly imagine a more repugnant place to spend an hour, much less eternity. But according to Jesus, such a place will be the eternal destination of the unrighteous.

The third word translated "hell" is the Greek word *Hades,* which Jesus employed in this story to describe the temporary location of the unsaved dead as they await the final Great White Throne Judgment described in Revelation 20:11-15. The Bible teaches that at that judgment, all the occupants of Hades will stand before God, and because their names are not found in the Book of Life—the record of all who have trusted in Christ as Savior—they will be cast into the lake of fire (Gehenna): "And if anyone's name was not found written in the book of life, he was thrown into the lake of fire" (verse 15).

Although, technically, Jesus was describing Hades in the story about the rich man and Lazarus, we can assume from His vivid descriptions that the temporary torment of Hades only foreshadows the eternal torment of the lake of fire (Gehenna). Therefore, I will use the term *hell* to describe both the temporary and eternal destination of the unrighteous.

Jesus firmly believed that hell is just as real a location as heaven. In John 14:2, Jesus promised His disciples, "I go to prepare a place for you." The Greek word for "place" is *topos,* which means "a geographical location." Heaven is not a state of mind, but it is the eternal destination for those who trust in Christ. In the same way, Jesus taught that hell was an actual destination rather than a state of mind. Read carefully how Jesus described the fate of the unrighteous: "These will go away into eternal punishment, but the righteous into eternal life" (Matthew 25:46).

My point is simply this: You can't have one group of people going to an actual location (heaven) and the other group of people going to a state of mind. Just as Jesus described heaven as a real place, He taught that hell is a real place.

Second, Jesus described hell as a place of horrendous suffering. In the above story, the rich man begged Abraham for relief because he was "in agony in this flame" (Luke 16:24). In Mark 9:48, Jesus also used the imagery of fire to describe the horrors of hell "where their worm does not die, and the fire is not quenched." Hell will also be a place of intense loneliness and sorrow where there will be continual "weeping and gnashing of teeth" (Matthew 22:13). Are we to believe that hell is a literal furnace in which a literal fire will continually burn the flesh of unbelievers for all eternity?

Dr. Albert Mohler, president of Southern Baptist Theological Seminary, thinks so. "Scripture clearly speaks of hell as a physical place of fiery torment and warns us we should fear."[11] However, others aren't so sure. Martin Luther and John Calvin, as well as Christian leaders of this age such as Francis Schaeffer and J. I. Packer, certainly believed in the reality of hell, but they view the fire as symbolic of God's eternal condemnation. A literal fire, they argue, is inconsistent with the description of the darkness of hell (see Matthew 22:13), and it also fails to allow for the degrees of punishment in hell that we will discuss in the next section.

However, even a symbolic understanding of the fiery torments Jesus described offers no real comfort to an unbeliever. If Jesus was speaking figuratively, He was saying that the pain of hell will be so horrendous that it defies description. The closest He was able to come to explaining the agony of hell was to compare it to flesh on fire for all eternity.

Third, Jesus taught that hell is a place of suffering forever. A growing number of Christians are embracing annihilationism, which postulates that unbelievers don't exist forever in hell as believers live forever in heaven. Instead, the unbeliever will be cast into the lake of fire where he or she will be destroyed. In other words, the only people who will live eternally are believers. There is no eternal punishment of unbelievers. According to this theory, regardless of how angry God is, He would not subject His creatures to everlasting torture. (To understand how long that would be, think in terms of billions of years.) Certainly, a loving and merciful God would not mete out such a harsh sentence.

Such a belief takes some of the sting out of hell. It offers some comfort to both unbelievers, who secretly wonder, "What if I'm wrong?" and Christians, who grieve over the fate of their non-Christian loved ones. But is there any biblical evidence for annihilationism?

Some would point to verses in the Bible, such as the following, which seem to indicate that unbelievers are destroyed rather than sentenced to eternal punishment:

> For God so loved the world, that He gave His only begotten Son, that whoever believes in Him shall not *perish*, but have eternal life. (John 3:16)

Do not fear those who kill the body but are unable to kill the soul; but rather fear Him who is able to *destroy* both soul and body in hell. (Matthew 10:28)

Admittedly, the words *perish* and *destroy* could be interpreted to mean that unbelievers simply cease to exist. However, these words can also be used to describe a process—a long process. For example, one could say, "The mountaineers perished from starvation" or "The heat destroyed the wood deck." In neither case did the destruction come immediately; rather, it occurred over a period of time.

When one interprets these verses in light of other scriptures, it becomes obvious that hell is forever. For example, Revelation 19:20 says that, upon the return of Christ, the Beast and the false prophet are "thrown alive into the lake of fire which burns with brimstone." Then, one thousand years later, the apostle John sees Satan being thrown into the same "lake of fire and brimstone, where the beast and the false prophet *are* also; and they will be tormented day and night forever and ever" (Revelation 20:10). Amazing! One thousand years after the Beast and the false prophet are thrown into the lake of fire, they are still alive and experiencing torment. Significantly, John used the same word to describe the eternality of hell that he also used to describe the eternality of heaven in Revelation 22:5: "forever."

In Matthew 25:46, Jesus drew a link not only between the reality of heaven and hell but also between the duration of heaven and hell: "These will go away into eternal punishment, but the righteous into eternal life." And in the story of the rich man and Lazarus, we see the rich man still alive while he is experiencing torment. The fiery judgment in this passage resulted in eternal pain, not immediate consumption.

How much weight should we give to Jesus's teachings about hell compared to the opinions of skeptics like Russell, Ingersoll, and others? Imagine that you are preparing for your first trip to England next March, and you are wondering what kind of clothing you should take on your journey. "Is it hot or cold, rainy or dry?" you muse aloud to your best friend.

"Oh, I imagine the weather is just like ours that time of year—moderate and dry," your friend replies.

The only problem is that your friend has never traveled outside the city limits. On the other hand, you encounter a clerk in your department store who has a strong English accent. After introducing yourself, you discover that she grew up in London, so you ask her for advice. "Oh no, it is freezing cold and damp that time of year. You had better dress very warmly."

Whose opinion are you going to trust?

When formulating our beliefs about hell, doesn't it seem wiser to trust the words of Someone who has seen life from the other side of the grave rather than the speculations of those who have never traveled outside this world? That drunk can bank on Ingersoll's opinion if he so chooses, but I think I'll go with Jesus.

I Know What the Bible Says, But...

In spite of the voluminous words of Jesus about both the reality and severity of hell, many dismiss the idea of eternal condemnation based on four common objections.

"God Is Too Loving to Send People to Hell"

Theologian Clark Pinnock frames the objection well: "How can Christians possibly project a deity of such cruelty and vindictiveness" that he inflicts "everlasting torture upon his creatures, however sinful they may have been?" Pinnock concludes that a God who would do such a thing is "more nearly like Satan than like God."[12] How could a God worthy of my love and respect torture men, women, and children for all eternity? Underneath that common objection are two presuppositions—both of which are fatally flawed.

First, the objection assumes that God is just as tolerant of sin as we are. In today's culture we think it is a virtue, not a vice, to be nonjudgmental and accepting of other people's flaws. So instead of turning away from immorality or violence, many of us turn toward it and tune in to it via television, movies, and the Internet. But our willingness to tolerate evil is due not to our righteousness, but to our unrighteousness. Our ability to dismiss sin in others as well as in ourselves is evidence of our unholiness, not our holiness.

But God is not like us. As He said through the psalmist, "You thought that I was just like you" (Psalm 50:21). Certainly there are many differences between God and us, but at the top of the list is God's inability to tolerate evil. Habakkuk described God as One whose "eyes are too pure to approve evil" and who cannot "look on wickedness with favor" (1:13).

Think about that for a moment. There is no one God the Father loves more than His own Son. Yet as Jesus Christ hung on the cross, carrying the sins of the world, God had to turn away from Him in disgust, causing Christ to cry out, "My God, My God, why have You forsaken Me?" (Matthew 27:46). If God cannot tolerate the sin borne by His own Son, how likely is He to tolerate sin in our lives?

God's holiness caused Him not only to turn away from Jesus, but also to condemn Him. Sin always demands God's punishment. Nahum 1:3 clearly states that the Lord "will by no means leave the guilty unpunished." And so, in some inexplicable way, Jesus Christ willingly accepted on our behalf the horrors of God's condemnation on the cross so that we might escape that same condemnation. If the Cross tells us anything, it reminds us that God has zero tolerance for sin.

Second the objection assumes that we really aren't *that* bad. As I've already stated, the majority of Americans believes that there needs to be a hell for extremely evil individuals such as Adolf Hitler, Ted Bundy, Charles Manson, or Jeffrey Dahlmer. But few people place themselves in that category. Instead, we tend to view ourselves as flawed, but certainly not deserving of eternal death. Our capacity for self-denial is unlimited.

James Hammond was a plantation owner during the Civil War who served as both a governor and a congressman. Besides defending the horrendous practice of slavery, Hammond was guilty of an unbridled sexual appetite. In 1839, Hammond purchased an eighteen-year-old slave named Sally, along with her infant daughter, Louisa. Hammond fathered several children by Sally, and then, when Louisa was twelve, he discarded Sally and fathered several more children through Louisa. His career in politics almost ended when Hammond's brother-in-law, Wade Hamilton, accused him of molesting Hamilton's four daughters, ages thirteen through eighteen.

But even more astonishing than James Hammond's horrendous sins was his ability to overlook his immorality. After his wife left him and he lost many of his slaves and livestock through sickness, Hammond wrote in his diary, "It crushes me to the earth to see every thing of mine so blasted around me. Negroes, cattle, mules, hogs, every thing that has life around me seems to labour under some fated malediction.... Great God, what have I done. Never was a man so cursed... what have I done or omitted to do to deserve this fate?"[13]

According to Jesus, similar cries of "righteous" indignation will pour forth from the lips of many on Judgment Day: "Lord, Lord, what have we done to deserve this?" they will argue (see Matthew 7:21-23). The truth is that we have all "missed the mark" (the meaning of the Greek word translated "sin"). Admittedly, some have missed it by a wider margin than others, but as Paul said, "All have sinned and fall short of the glory of God" (Romans 3:23).

The geographical distance between the North Pole and the South Pole is great but also negligible when compared to the distance between the earth and the farthest star in the universe. Similarly, the moral difference between Mother Teresa (as well as you and me) and Adolf Hitler is insignificant compared to the distance between us and God. We have all fallen woefully short.

Once we understand—really understand—the great moral gulf between God and us, then Hell does not seem so unreasonable. D. A. Carson has said:

> Hell is not a place where people are consigned because
> they were pretty good blokes but just didn't believe the right
> stuff. They're consigned there, first and foremost, because they
> defy their Maker and want to be at the center of the universe.
> Hell is not filled with people who have already repented, only
> God isn't gentle enough or good enough to let them out. It's
> filled with people who, for all eternity, still want to be at the
> center of the universe and who persist in their God-defying
> rebellion.
>
>   What is God to do? If he says it doesn't matter to him, then
> God is no longer a God to be admired. He's either amoral or
> positively creepy. For him to act in any other way in the face of
> such blatant defiance would be to reduce God himself.[14]

"Hell Is Too Severe a Punishment for Wrong Beliefs"

Even if we accept God's holiness and our sinfulness, we still have to wonder if God isn't overreacting by condemning people to hell just because they rejected Jesus Christ as their Savior. How could such a mistake warrant eternal condemnation? Are we really prepared to say that a moral Muslim who loves his family and tries his best to keep what he understands to be God's laws is deserving of the same fate as a man who abuses, tortures, and butchers little children?

The author of Hebrews explains that rejecting—or simply neglecting—Christ is not as innocuous as one might think. Listen to his description of what a person is *really* doing when he or she fails to respond to the gospel:

> How much severer punishment do you think he will deserve
> who has trampled under foot the Son of God, and has regarded
> as unclean the blood of the covenant by which he was sanctified,
> and has insulted the Spirit of grace? (Hebrews 10:29)

The person who fails to trust in Christ is, first of all, guilty of "tramp[ling] under foot the Son of God." The Greek verb *katapateo* (translated "trampled") was frequently used to describe salt, which, after losing its flavor, would be thrown onto the road and trampled by the travelers' feet. The salt was discarded because it was considered worthless. Similarly, the person who rejects, or even neglects, the gospel is rendering Christ's horrific death on the cross meaningless. That person's attitude is like that of media mogul Ted Turner who described Christianity as "a religion for losers." At a meeting at the Carter Center in Atlanta, Georgia, Turner told a group that Jesus did not need to die for him: "I don't want anybody to die for me. I've had a few drinks and a few girlfriends, and if that's gonna put me in hell, well, then so be it."

But it gets worse. The writer of Hebrews says that the one who fails to accept God's gift of forgiveness through Christ judges Christ's blood as "unclean." The word translated "unclean" is related to the Jewish pronouncements that Gentiles were "unclean" and were no better than the mongrel dogs that roamed the streets of Jerusalem. So when an unbeliever rejects Christ, he or she is essentially saying, "Jesus's blood has no more value than the blood of an animal."

Surely such an assessment would be grounds for God to give up on unbelievers and send them to their deserved fate. But God doesn't give up. His Spirit continues to plead with unbelievers to trust in Christ for their salvation. Yet in spite of the Spirit's invitation to salvation, the unbeliever's response is to "insult the Spirit of grace." The word translated "insult" means "to treat in a spiteful manner." Perhaps this illustration will help you grasp what the writer of Hebrews had in mind.

Imagine that you look out your window and notice that your neighbor's front yard is flooding due to a broken water main. You send your son over to inform the neighbor of the problem. When your son attempts to explain why he is there, the neighbor responds, "You snotty-nosed, worthless kid! I don't need you to tell me anything. Get off my property now!" Although you are angry about the mistreatment of your son, you still feel sorry for your neighbor who is about to suffer a flooded yard and an inflated water bill, so you send over your mate to warn him. This time his response is even more harsh. He calls your mate every name in the book and threatens to have your mate arrested for trespassing if he or she doesn't leave immediately. After your neighbor insults both your son and your mate, how likely are you to offer him any more assistance?[15]

The non-Christian has, in effect, labeled the death of God's Son "worthless." Additionally, he or she continually insults God's Spirit by rejecting His repeated invitations to salvation. Is it really that difficult to see why the unbeliever is deserving of God's judgment?

Ultimately, every occupant of hell will be there by his own choice.

"It Is Unfair to Condemn Those Who Have Never Had the Chance to Believe in Jesus"

Is it right for God to send a ten-year-old African girl to hell just because she has never heard of Jesus Christ? And to push the question a little further, is it just for God to sentence her to the same kind of punishment as a ruthless murderer? Some would answer those questions by simply quoting Romans 9:14—"There is no injustice with God, is there?"—and leaving it at that. Admittedly, such a statement is true, but I think there are some better ways to answer the skeptic's argument.

First, the objection assumes the innocence of the little girl. Yet, the Bible says that she—along with everyone else on the planet—is guilty of sin and is deserving of eternal death. Paul pronounced God's indictment against the entire human race with this quotation from Psalm 14: "There is none righteous, not even one" (Romans 3:10). But what has this little ten-year-old girl done that is so bad? Is arguing with your parents, stealing a banana from a neighbor's tree, or hitting your little brother so terrible that it warrants eternal damnation? Remember, God is not like us. Our ability to tolerate the peccadilloes of others is evidence not of our goodness, but of our badness. God has no tolerance for evil, and He must judge it.

Thus, if that little girl and every other person on the planet are guilty and deserving of God's eternal condemnation, the question changes from "Why doesn't God save everyone?" to "Why does God save *anyone?*" For example, imagine that the president of the United States pardons an individual from death row due to extenuating circumstances surrounding the case. Some may not agree with the president's decision, but does anyone accuse him of being unmerciful because he did not pardon *every* prisoner on death row? The fact that he pardoned one person is evidence of the president's compassion, not cruelty.

In the same way, every human creature has been declared guilty, has been sentenced to eternal death, and is simply awaiting final execution in the lake of fire. Those whom God pardons are the recipients of His mercy, and those who experience hell are the recipients of His justice. But neither group is treated unjustly.

Second, the skeptic's objection assumes that the little girl has no chance to be saved. However, as we saw earlier, God has revealed to this little girl (and to every other human being) the truth of His existence through nature. On a moonlit African night, she can look up into the sky and know there must be a Creator. While a belief in God alone is not enough to save that ten-year-old girl, it is a starting place for her to receive a deeper understanding of God. The examples of Cornelius and the Ethiopian eunuch strongly suggest that those who respond to such a basic knowledge of God will be given further insight into the gospel of Christ.

I should stop here and point out another popular answer to the question, How are those who never heard the gospel saved? Some evangelical Christians who reject universalism (the belief that God will save everyone regardless of their belief or unbelief) embrace the concept of the "noble pagan." They contend that people today, who, like this African girl, have never heard of Christ, can be saved in the same way that the Old Testament believers were saved. Sir Norman Anderson, a proponent of this view, says that in the Old Testament a person was saved by acknowledging his sinfulness, abandoning any attempt to earn his own forgiveness, and instead trusting in God's provision for salvation. "The believing Jew was accepted and blessed not because of the prescribed animal sacrifices he offered, not even [because of] his repentance and abandonment to God's mercy, but because of what God Himself was going to do in His only Son at the cross of Calvary."[16] Likewise, Anderson argues, people who have never heard of Christ can be saved in the same manner as the Old Testament believers who were saved "on credit."

Think of it this way: When you go to a department store and purchase a sweater, you hand the clerk a piece of plastic called a credit card, and the clerk gives you a valuable sweater. Why would any store allow you to receive valuable merchandise in exchange for showing a piece of plastic? Because that credit card represents a promise to pay. Thirty days later the bill arrives, and (hopefully) you will pay it. Now the exchange is complete. In the same way, the Old Testament believers were saved "on credit." The offering of sacrifices was like putting down a credit card. There was nothing in those sacrifices that earned the believers eternal life, but that act of faith was a promise to pay. And thousands of years later, when Christ died on the cross, He paid the bill in full.

How was the Old Testament believer saved? How can the African girl who has never heard the gospel be saved? How are you and I saved? The very same way: through the death of Christ for our sins. Those of us who have heard about Christ and reject Him have no hope of forgiveness. But it is unclear how much the Old Testament believer who had never heard about Jesus or the African girl today who has never been exposed to the gospel must understand in order to be saved. Regardless of the answer, we can trust God to do the right thing.

Finally, as to the fate of those who have never heard the gospel, the Bible clearly teaches that there will be degrees of hell just as there will be degrees of heaven. Will that ten-year-old girl who has never heard of Christ but rejects the revelation she has received suffer the same fate as a mass murderer or one who contemptuously rejects Christ? Absolutely not! Hell will not be the same for everyone. We will be judged according to our response to the knowledge we have received, as Paul explained in Romans 2:12: "All who have sinned without the Law will also perish without the Law, and all who have sinned under the Law will be judged by the Law."

Paul was saying that the Jew (and, by extension, the Christian) who has possession of God's Word will be judged more severely than someone who has not received the full revelation of God. Both groups of unbelievers will spend eternity in hell, but some will be judged more harshly than others.

Jesus also taught that there will be degrees of hell based on the revelation we have received:

> And that slave who knew his master's will and did not get ready
> or act in accord with his will, will receive many lashes, but the
> one who did not know it, and committed deeds worthy of a
> flogging, will receive but few. (Luke 12:47-48)

The fact that there will be degrees of hell should offer little consolation to unbelievers for two reasons. First, those who receive only a "few" lashes will still be separated from God for all eternity. The chasm between heaven and hell is tremendous, regardless of the degree to which you are experiencing either. Second, and most significant, those unbelievers who have heard about "degrees of hell" have obviously received a fuller knowledge of God's revelation and are therefore subject to the severest of God's judgments. In other words, the fact that a person knows about a "lesser hell" disqualifies her from experiencing it!

These three responses to the skeptic's objection simply underscore this basic truth about God: He is just and can be trusted to do what is right.

"How Can Anyone Enjoy Heaven if People Are Burning in Hell?"

Let me answer that question with another question. Think about the best meal you've ever eaten. I'm talking about a thick, juicy steak and baked potato dripping with butter and sour cream, topped off by a piece of homemade pecan pie with a scoop of vanilla ice cream. (You can tell I'm a Texan.) If that's not your idea of a fine dinner, then travel back in your mind to the best meal you've ever savored. Have it in mind? Now here's the question: How could you have enjoyed that dinner knowing that more than a billion people in the world—men, women, children, and little babies—are going to bed hungry every night? Did that thought even cross your mind while you were wolfing down your meal? And if your answer is yes, how long did you dwell on such a thought?

"But, Robert," you argue, "that illustration is flawed. Admittedly, in this world people are selfish, but in heaven people will be like Christ. Surely those in heaven will have compassion on those who are in hell. How could heaven be enjoyed if loved ones on earth—friends, parents, or even our children—were being tormented in hell? Won't we weep over their fate just as Jesus wept over the city of Jerusalem?"

Those who have believed in Christ on earth *will* indeed be like Christ in heaven, but nothing in heaven or hell will extinguish Christ's joy—or ours. Although Jesus wept over the fate of the lost while He was on earth, when He comes again He will, without any hint of remorse or regret, pronounce the final sentence on all who have rejected Him (see Revelation 20:11-15). He will deal out "retribution to those who do not know God and to those who do not obey the gospel of our Lord Jesus" (2 Thessalonians 1:8). Furthermore, Christ will "be marveled at among all who have believed" (2 Thessalonians 1:10). That is, every believer will fully comprehend and agree with His verdict against all unbelievers—including our loved ones.

Although that truth is hard to fathom, J. I. Packer offers some helpful words:

> Remember, in heaven our minds, hearts, motives, and feelings
> will be sanctified, so that we are fully conformed to the character
> and outlook of Jesus our Lord.... In heaven, glorifying God and
> thanking him for everything will always absorb us. All our love
> for and joy in others who are with us in heaven will spring from
> their doing the same, and love and pity for hell's occupants will
> not enter our hearts. Their hell will not veto our heaven.[17]

A FINAL THOUGHT ABOUT A FIERY HELL

Many Christians seem embarrassed about hell. They refrain from speaking about it to non-Christians lest they be branded as fire-and-brimstone Bible-thumpers. To warn people that they are in danger of eternal torment unless they trust in Christ as Savior seems unsophisticated and unloving. But by omitting the subject of hell from conversations with those who don't believe, Christians are—perhaps unconsciously—elevating themselves above Jesus Christ. Given Jesus's numerous and unapologetic warnings about Hell, can anyone assume that he or she is more educated and compassionate than He is?

Jesus's motivation for proclaiming the severity of hell was not to condemn people, but to save people from this awful inevitability. Remember what He said?

> For God did not send the Son into the world to judge the world, but that the world might be saved through Him.... He who does not believe has been judged already, because he has not believed in the name of the only begotten Son of God. (John 3:17-18)

We were all under a death sentence before Christ appeared. His purpose in coming was to offer us a way out.

Imitating Jesus's style, His followers should compassionately but boldly remind unbelievers of the severe consequences of unbelief. To omit hell from a discussion with a non-Christian is to miss the greatest incentive a person has for becoming a Christian.

Larry Dixon came to that realization through an encounter with a truckdriver:

> I remember during my seminary years getting stuck in a Pennsylvania snowstorm. As I sat in a diner waiting for my car to be rescued from a snow bank, I started talking with a truck driver about the gospel. When I told him about the love of Christ, he stifled several yawns and said he wasn't interested in religion.
>
> Then it dawned on me that I should talk to him about hell. I told him how I deserved to go there, but that Jesus Christ had taken the punishment of my sin upon Himself when He died for me. The trucker hung on my every word.
>
> I wish I could say he trusted Christ on the spot. He didn't. But at least I warned him—and he listened.[18]

In a misguided attempt to be relevant and more sensitive to the needs of non-Christians, some have modified the gospel message dramatically. Instead of saying that "Jesus came to save us from hell," many talk about Jesus's ability to "save" us from loneliness, lack of purpose, or a poor self-image. Such a seemingly innocuous shift of emphasis eliminates the most potent reason anyone has for trusting in Christ. As John Gerstner says, "The fear of hell is the only thing most likely to get worldly people thinking about the kingdom of God. No rational human being can be convinced that he is in imminent danger of everlasting torment and do nothing about it!"[19]

Is there a hell? Yes! And as theologian Martin Marty once said, "If people really believed in hell, they wouldn't be watching basketball games or even the TV preachers. They'd be out rescuing people."[20]

Homosexuality Is a Perversion

I hesitated for a few moments after typing this chapter title, wondering if I really wanted to use the words *homosexuality* and *perversion* in the same sentence. After all, in today's culture, those who make such declarations are automatically stereotyped by the media as hatemongers whose language incites people to acts of violence against homosexuals. Consequently, opponents of homosexuality are blamed for the violence perpetrated against gays. The blood of homosexuals who are beaten or killed is said to be on the hands of those who dare suggest that there is something abnormal and abominable about same-sex intercourse. By the way, I'm not speaking hypothetically, but from personal experience.

A few years ago I was nestled in my favorite chair with a bowl of popcorn watching a rerun of *Columbo* on the A&E (Arts and Entertainment) cable network. During the commercial break, there was a promo for an upcoming special about the relationship between "hate speech" and violence against homosexuals. I just about flipped over my bowl of popcorn when I saw a clip of me preaching fervently against homosexuality, calling it "an abomination." As you might expect, the network hooked at least one viewer with that enticing commercial!

A few nights later I tuned in to the documentary with some trepidation. The host first recounted one gruesome crime after another that had been committed against gays, culminating with the famous case of

Matthew Shepard, the teenage homosexual who was crucified on a fence post in Wyoming in 1998 by a group of gay bashers. Then came a shot of yours truly proclaiming that "homosexuality is an abomination against God." Also included were video clips of Pastor Fred Phelps in a white cowboy hat protesting at Shepard's funeral. Holding a fluorescent sign of Matthew Shepard's face amid the blood red flames of hell, he chanted, "Matt is in hell." Television makes for strange bedfellows.

The twofold implication was clear. First, anyone who is critical of homosexuality is guilty of hate speech regardless of whether he or she is preaching in a pulpit or protesting at a funeral. Second, such hate speech is directly responsible for brutality against gays. The conclusion? If we are going to stamp out prejudice and violence against gays in our society, we must silence those who are critical of homosexuality. And there is a concerted effort to do just that.

Dr. Charles W. Socarides, clinical professor of psychiatry at Albert Einstein College of Medicine in New York and president of the National Association for Research and Therapy of Homosexuality, describes the brilliant plan presented in Marshall Kirk and Hunter Madsen's book *After the Ball* that would "normalize the abnormal" practice of homosexuality by utilizing the same brainwashing techniques employed by the Chinese.[1]

The first step is to desensitize the public to homosexuality by demonstrating that gays are just like everyone else.[2] If you can laugh with smart, attractive, and witty gays such as Will, the main character on television's *Will and Grace,* or if you sympathize with characters such as the homosexual attorney dying from AIDS in the movie *Philadelphia,* then you can hardly be frightened or repulsed by them.

The second step is to "jam" the public by causing people to feel guilty about their bigotry toward homosexuals.[3] When opponents of homosexuality are stereotyped as shrill, uneducated bigots, and then depicted as being shunned by those in mainstream society, opponents will naturally think, *My gosh, I don't want to be like* that!

The final step is conversion during which masses of people change their attitudes about homosexuality "through a planned psychological attack, in the form of propaganda fed to the nation via the media."[4]

How successful has the conversion of American attitudes concerning homosexuality been? I could cite statistics about the ever-increasing acceptance of homosexuality by Americans in general and by Christians in particular. But the following paragraph concerning the abnormality of homosexuality illustrates the point even more effectively:

> Even in purely nonreligious terms, homosexuality represents a misuse of the sexual faculty and, in the words of one...educator, of "human construction." It is a pathetic little second-rate substitute for reality, a pitiable flight from life. As such it deserves fairness, compassion, understanding and, when possible, treatment. But it deserves no encouragement, no glamorization, no rationalization, no fake status as minority martyrdom.[5]

Would you like to guess the source of that quote? *Christianity Today?* Wrong. Focus on the Family? Wrong again. It came from *Time* magazine, January 21, 1966. Can you imagine the outrage today if a major news magazine published an article labeling homosexuality as "pathetic" and "pitiable" and condemned efforts to give it "fake status as a minority martyrdom"? Yet, as recently as 1972, the American Psychiatric Association (APA) treated homosexuality as a disorder deserving of psychiatric treatment.

But in a stroke of genius, those intent on converting America's attitudes toward gays were able to convince the APA to no longer refer to homosexuality as a "disorder," but rather, "a condition" like being left-handed.[6] In time, it was no longer homosexuals who needed therapy, but those who opposed it. Literally. According to California State law,

- "All K–12 schoolchildren must be taught to 'appreciate' various sexual orientations."
- "Public-school teachers and counselors must identify children with the potential to be 'intolerant' of homosexuality—and refer them for retraining."
- "School sports teams that object to homosexual or transsexual behavior may be barred from participating in California Inter-scholastic Federation sports."
- "Nonprofit groups such as the Boy Scouts that refuse to hire homosexuals may be fined up to $150,000 per incident."[7]

I would say that the plan of desensitizing, jamming, and converting has been wildly successful, wouldn't you?

But God's Word has not changed. The Bible describes homosexuality as a perversion of God's design for human sexuality that has devastating physical, emotional, and spiritual consequences. Christians should not fall into the trap of cutting our consciences to fit this year's fashion, to paraphrase American playwright Lillian Hellman. Homosexuality is a distortion of God's plan for human sexuality.

Yet, I believe there is a better way to uphold this politically incorrect truth than by picketing with a "God Hates Faggots" sign at a homosexual's funeral service. As I wrote this chapter, I was reminded again of the need to mix hard truth with tender love when dealing with this volatile subject.

An Unexpected Call

I had carefully read and organized dozens of articles from medical journals and popular magazines in preparation for writing this chapter.

With my research complete and my outline formulated, I was ready to begin writing when my secretary informed me there was an urgent call I needed to take. More than a little perturbed at the interruption, I took the call and was immediately glad I did. On the other end of the phone was a leader in the church—and a close personal friend—whose voice betrayed his desperation.

"Robert, our daughter Susan has just announced to us that she is gay. We don't know what to do. Can we bring her in tomorrow afternoon to talk with you?"

After expressing my sincere sorrow over the situation and assuring him that they were not the first Christian parents to confront such a crisis, I asked, "Does Susan want to visit with me?" (Silent pause as father attempts to keep from hurting pastor's feelings.)

"Well, not exactly. But we told her she had to come."

I could hardly wait for the appointment.

The next afternoon Susan, an attractive and articulate high-school senior, came into my office. I remembered years earlier when she had made her profession of faith in Christ and I had baptized her.

"You really don't want to be here, do you?" I asked.

She shook her head.

I assured her of the confidentiality of our conversation and began by assessing her spiritual condition. Perhaps Susan really was not a Christian and that explained her homosexual behavior. "If you were standing before God and He were to ask you, 'Why should I let you into heaven?' what would you say?"

Without a moment's hesitation, she answered, "Because I've trusted in Christ as my Savior." *Strike one.*

"Let me ask you a personal but very important question. Were you ever molested as a child?"

"No, never," she answered. *Strike two.*

Since Susan had been reared in a strong Christian home and had been actively involved in an evangelical church that emphasized biblical doctrine, certainly she must feel some conflict about her actions. "How do you think God feels about your homosexual activity?"

After a momentary hesitation, she said, "I understand now that God created me with these desires, desires that I have had since I was a little girl. For years I have been miserable trying to deny those feelings and have seriously contemplated suicide. But now that I have accepted who I am, I am happier than I have ever been in my life!" *Strike three.*

What does one say to a Christian who seems completely at peace about his or her homosexuality? Obviously, the first step is to turn to the Bible and point out how homosexual behavior is contrary to Scripture. I did just that. But every argument I presented was refuted by a powerful rebuttal. For the last several days I had been preparing to write a chapter in a book—or so I thought. But in reality God had been equipping me with the ammunition I needed not to win an argument, but to help rescue one of His children from the clutches of the Enemy.

That afternoon Susan articulated seven of the most popular myths about homosexuality that both believers and unbelievers are increasingly embracing.

Myth one: "The only prohibitions against homosexuality are in the Old Testament and therefore are not applicable today." Several years ago on an episode of *The West Wing,* fictional president Jeb Bartlett confronted a popular radio psychologist, known for her stance against homosexuality, at a White House reception. (The psychologist, incidentally, was patterned after radio's Dr. Laura Schlessinger.) The exchange went something like this:

PRESIDENT: "I understand that you think homosexuality is a sin."

DR. LAURA LOOK-ALIKE: "That's right. The Scriptures say homosexuality is an abomination against God."

PRESIDENT: "What Scripture are you talking about?"

DR. LAURA LOOK-ALIKE: "Leviticus 18:22 says, 'You shall not lie with a male as he lies with a female; it is an abomination.'"

PRESIDENT: "I understand you enjoy football. Yet every time your favorite team touches the ball made of pigskin, they violate Leviticus 7:21: 'And when anyone touches anything unclean, whether human uncleanness or an unclean animal...that person shall be cut off from his people.' And by the way, the outfit you are wearing tonight is an abomination to God according to Leviticus 19:19, since it consists of two kinds of material mixed together. Why do you hold on to one verse of Leviticus and dismiss the others as being irrelevant?"

Good question, President Bartlett. In fact, no sooner had that scene faded to a commercial than my phone began ringing with calls from church members wanting to know how to answer his question!

First, let's give the fictional president credit for knowing his Bible. It is true that as Christians we no longer live under Old Testament laws. The purpose of those regulations was to separate Israel from heathen nations. One way the Israelites demonstrated their distinctiveness was by abstaining from practices common among unbelievers such as eating "unclean" animals, wearing two kinds of material, engaging in homosexual behavior, piercing or tattooing the body, practicing incest, or shaving around the temples or the ears. Obviously, some of those behaviors were inherently evil, and others were not. So how do we decide which of those laws we will obey today and which we will ignore?

The answer is quite easy. We turn to the New Testament and use it as a guide for our behavior. The new "testament" (meaning "agreement") we now live under retains the moral laws of the Old Testament but discards most of the ceremonial and civil regulations that were peculiar to Israel. For example, Jesus reaffirmed each of the Ten

Commandments except one: "Observe the Sabbath day by keeping it holy." Why did He omit that commandment? As Christians we no longer observe the ceremonial worship laws designed for the Israelites, which included worshiping on the seventh day, Saturday. Instead, the early Christians began worshiping on the first day of the week in honor of Christ's resurrection from the dead.

So the real question for Christians is, Does the *New Testament* have any prohibitions against homosexuality? And the answer is yes. Consider the following scriptures:

> For this reason God gave them over to degrading passions; for their women exchanged the natural function for that which is unnatural, and in the same way also the men abandoned the natural function of the woman and burned in their desire toward one another, men with men committing indecent acts and receiving in their own persons the due penalty of their error. (Romans 1:26-27)

> Or do you not know that the unrighteous will not inherit the kingdom of God? Do not be deceived; neither fornicators, nor idolaters, nor adulterers, nor effeminate, nor homosexuals, nor thieves, nor the covetous, nor drunkards, nor revilers, nor swindlers, will inherit the kingdom of God. (1 Corinthians 6:9-10)

> But we know that the Law is good, if one uses it lawfully, realizing the fact that law is not made for a righteous person, but for those who are lawless and rebellious, for the ungodly and sinners, for the unholy and profane, for those who kill their fathers

or mothers, for murderers and immoral men and homosexuals
and kidnappers and liars and perjurers, and whatever else is
contrary to sound teaching. (1 Timothy 1:8-10)

When confronted with such verses, the homosexual advocate usually resorts to the second myth.

Myth two: "Jesus never condemned homosexuality." As a result of the
events I described at the beginning of this book, I found myself on the
witness stand in a federal lawsuit against our city. At issue was a city res-
olution we had supported allowing citizens to have library books they
deemed objectionable moved from the children's section to the adult
section of the library (not banned or burned, but simply moved). Since
the two books that generated the compromise, *Heather Has Two Mommies* and *Daddy's Roommate,* were prohomosexual books, the lawyer for
the ACLU wanted to demonstrate that my stand against these books
was rooted in bigotry, not the Bible. Like many people, the attorney
knew just enough about the Bible to be dangerous—to himself.

"Tell me, Dr. Jeffress," he asked as he paced in front of the witness
stand. "What did Jesus have to say about homosexuality?"

Of course, I was supposed to hang my head in shame and say,
"Nothing," proving how unlike Jesus I was in my prejudice against gays.
But I didn't answer that way. Instead I replied, "Actually, Jesus had quite
a bit to say about homosexuality."

The attorney raised an eyebrow and said, "Oh, really? Like what?"
he asked, hoping he had caught me in a perjurious statement.

I replied by quoting the above verses from Romans, 1 Corinthians,
and 1 Timothy.

"But Jesus didn't say those things," he protested. "Paul did."

"That's right. But as Christians we believe that all Scripture is inspired by God. And since we also believe that Jesus is equal to God, then these are Jesus's words as well."

Actually, the argument that Jesus never condemned homosexuality is flawed in at least three ways. First, it assumes that Jesus's words are more authoritative than the rest of the Bible—something that the Bible itself never claims. Instead, the Bible says that "all Scripture is inspired by God" (2 Timothy 3:16). The phrase "inspired by God" comes from one Greek word *theospnuestos,* which means "God-breathed." Every word in the Bible, from Genesis to the maps (just kidding), originated with God.

Second, how do we know that Jesus never said anything against homosexuality? Although the Bible is a *true* record of all that Jesus said, it is not a *complete* record of all that He said or did. The gospel writer John concluded his gospel by noting, "And there are also many other things which Jesus did, which if they were written in detail, I suppose that even the world itself would not contain the books that would be written" (John 21:25).

Finally, Jesus *did* condemn homosexuality by upholding God's pattern for human sexuality. When the Pharisees questioned the Lord about the thorny issue of divorce, Jesus referred them back to the Creation story to remind them of God's original design:

> And He answered and said, "Have you not read that He who
> created them from the beginning made them male and female,
> and said, 'For this reason a man shall leave his father and mother
> and be joined to his wife, and the two shall become one flesh'?
> So they are no longer two, but one flesh. What therefore God
> has joined together, let no man separate." (Matthew 19:4-6)

These brief verses remind us that God intended sex to be practiced in a marriage relationship ("shall...be joined to his wife," not "to his significant other"), a monogamous relationship ("let no man separate"), and most obvious, a male-female relationship ("made them male and female"). Yes, I know it sounds like something you might read on Pastor Fred Phelps's placard, but it is nevertheless true: God created Adam and Eve, not Adam and Steve.

As far as we know, Jesus never directly addressed the issue of homosexuality, just as He never addressed bestiality, incest, pedophilia, necrophilia, or any other sexual aberration. He didn't need to. By affirming God's original design for human sexuality, He automatically condemned any deviation from that standard.

As I write these words, our nation is debating the issue of gay marriage. Due to the illegal actions of local officials in California, New Mexico, and other states in issuing thousands of marriage licenses to homosexual couples, the president of the United States has announced his support for a constitutional amendment defining marriage as a union between one man and one woman. Such an amendment is necessary, the president claims, "To prevent the meaning of marriage from being changed forever."[8] Lesbian activist and former talk-show host Rosie O'Donnell, who announced her intentions to marry her female lover after the president's announcement, called his support for the traditional definition of marriage "the most vile and hurtful words ever spoken by a sitting president. I am stunned and I am horrified."[9]

Yet O'Donnell apparently is unaware of the fact that the president is simply repeating the teachings of Jesus Christ who declared unequivocally that marriage is reserved for a man and a woman. Period. Would O'Donnell call Jesus a hatemonger for making such a declaration?

But what is wrong with allowing those who don't accept Jesus's teachings to enjoy the legal benefits of marriage? Why shouldn't Christians just "live and let live"? Because to alter the definition of marriage is to devalue marriage. For example, suppose that society determines that the word *purple* should no longer be restricted to describing what has been traditionally thought of as the color purple, but instead, *purple* can now be used to describe every hue and tint in the earth. An apple, a daisy, the sky, and autumn leaves are all declared to be *purple*. Suddenly, the color purple has lost its distinctiveness.

If we start describing an immoral relationship between two men or between two women as *marriage,* what prevents society from stopping there? Suppose three men and a woman or a man and his nineteen-year-old daughter or a woman and her beloved cat decide they want to be "married," why should society deprive them of that right?

Once government starts labeling any and every relationship as *marriage,* it has not only created confusion as the president declared, but it has also devalued a relationship that Jesus taught is reserved for one man and one woman.

Myth three: "The Bible's condemnation of homosexuality is based on a misunderstanding of the text." Non-Christian homosexuals will not be fazed by the Bible's strident condemnation of homosexual behavior. To them, the Bible is just a collection of human musings about God and has no more authority than Aesop's fables. But those homosexuals who profess to be Christians must find a way to reconcile Scripture with homosexual practice. Let's look at three of the most well-known biblical injunctions against homosexuality and see how homosexual advocates "interpret" them:

1. God's destruction of Sodom (Genesis 19). Two angels went to visit the notoriously wicked city of Sodom to determine whether to spare it from God's judgment. These two angelic visitors, appearing as men, stayed with Lot, the nephew of Abraham:

Before [the angels] lay down, the men of the city, the men of Sodom, surrounded the house, both young and old, all the people from every quarter; and they called to Lot and said to him, "Where are the men who came to you tonight? Bring them out to us that we may have [sexual] relations with them." But Lot went out to them at the doorway, and shut the door behind him, and said, "Please, my brothers, do not act wickedly."… Then the two men [angels] said to Lot, "Whom else have you here?… Whomever you have in the city, bring them out of the place; for we are about to destroy this place, because their outcry has become so great before the LORD that the LORD has sent us to destroy it." (verses 4-7,12-13)

Some argue that these residents of Sodom were only interested in an innocent let's-get-to-know-one-another gathering with these angelic visitors. But the word translated "know" in some versions clearly means "to have sexual relations with." Otherwise why would Lot characterize their request as "wicked"? Obviously, the angels felt that these men had more in mind than attending a social mixer since the angels "struck the men who were at the doorway of the house with blindness" (verse 11).

Others will argue that the sin condemned in this passage was not homosexuality, but rape. In other words, God did not judge Sodom for homosexual activity, but for *forced* homosexual activity. As Joe Dallas, founder of Genesis Counseling, points out, there is an element of truth to this argument. However, the fact that the mob included "both young and old, all the people from every quarter" (verse 4) demonstrates how pervasive homosexuality was throughout the city. Extrabiblical literature such as the writings of Philo and Josephus cite homosexual conduct as the chief behavior for which Sodom was known.[10]

Still others argue that some passages of Scripture attribute Sodom's destruction to a lack of concern for the needy rather than to homosexuality. For example, they cite Ezekiel 16:49: "This was the guilt of your sister Sodom: she and her daughters had arrogance, abundant food and careless ease, but she did not help the poor and needy." If homosexuality were the primary sin, why didn't God mention it here? Again, there is a kernel of truth in this argument. Certainly Sodom's sins were not limited to homosexuality and included the arrogance that evidenced itself by insensitivity to the needs of others. But that same arrogance was also directed toward God's laws and led to sexual sin, as seen in the next verse: "Thus they were haughty and committed abominations before Me. Therefore I removed them when I saw it" (Ezekiel 16:50). Other passages also indicate that sexual perversion was a chief reason for Sodom's destruction:

> And if He condemned the cities of Sodom and Gomorrah to destruction by reducing them to ashes, having made them an example to those who would live ungodly lives thereafter; and if He rescued righteous Lot, oppressed by the sensual conduct of unprincipled men... (2 Peter 2:6-7)

> Just as Sodom and Gomorrah and the cities around them, since they in the same way as these indulged in gross immorality and went after strange flesh, are exhibited as an example in undergoing the punishment of eternal fire. (Jude 7)

While Sodom's sins were many, it is significant that this attempted homosexual attack was the final straw that resulted in God's destruction of the city.

2. The condemnation of homosexuality as an "abomination" (Leviticus 18; 20). Yesterday I accidentally took a telephone call from an irate television viewer who said, "If I ever hear you call something an 'abomination' again, I'm going to turn off the television." I gently explained that I was simply repeating what God had said. "I have a damn Bible. I can read for myself without your telling me what it says," the gentle soul replied. Fair enough. Let's allow the Bible to speak for itself:

> You shall not lie with a male as one lies with a female; it is an *abomination*. (Leviticus 18:22)

> If a man lies with a male as he lies with a woman, both of them have committed an *abomination*. They shall surely be put to death. Their blood shall be upon them. (Leviticus 20:13, NKJV)

As I explained earlier, some get around these verses by simply pointing out that they are part of the Old Covenant, which, they argue, is not applicable to Christians today. But another popular interpretation among gay theologians involves associating "abomination" with idolatry. Since Leviticus also uses the word *abomination* to describe idolatry, they claim that the real sin involved here is not homosexuality, but homosexuality that is used as a religious ritual in the worship of pagan gods. However, there are at least two problems with that interpretation. First, the other kinds of sexual immorality prohibited in these verses, such as bestiality and incest, had nothing to do with idolatry. Also, the word *abomination* is used elsewhere in Scripture to describe behavior that has no association with idolatry. For example, in Proverbs 6 the writer described seven "abominations" to the Lord such as pride and lying. None of the seven sins mentioned in that passage is associated with idolatry.

3. Paul's condemnation of homosexuality (Romans 1). Let's look again at Paul's description of homosexuality in Romans 1:

For this reason God gave them over to degrading passions; for
their women exchanged the natural function for that which is
unnatural, and in the same way also the men abandoned the
natural function of the woman and burned in their desire
toward one another, men with men committing indecent acts
and receiving in their own persons the due penalty of their error.
(verses 26-27)

While such a denunciation seems clear, the homosexual apologist
points out that the context of Romans 1 is idolatry. The people Paul had
in mind were those who rejected the knowledge of the true God and
instead created their own gods in the images of "corruptible man and of
birds and four-footed animals and crawling creatures" (verse 23). Thus,
once again the real sin in view here, they claim, is not homosexuality,
but idolatry. The Christian homosexual who worships the true God is
not condemned.

While it is true that Paul was describing those who have received,
rejected, and replaced the knowledge of the true God with a god of their
own creation, this does not diminish the sting of Paul's indictment of
homosexuality—in fact, it increases it. Paul labeled homosexual practice
as an "impurity" (verse 24) and described homosexual desires as "degrading passions" (verse 26). Moreover, Paul claimed that homosexuality is
God's judgment against those who engage in idolatry: "Therefore God
gave them over in the lusts of their hearts to impurity" (verse 24).

Additionally, if Paul were condemning only homosexuality when it
is practiced by idolaters, then the same standard must apply to other
behaviors mentioned in this same passage:

And just as they did not see fit to acknowledge God any longer,
God gave them over to a depraved mind, to do those things

which are not proper, being filled with all unrighteousness,
wickedness, greed, evil; full of envy, murder, strife, deceit,
malice; they are gossips... (verses 28-29)

Does anyone really want to argue that greed, envy, and murder
are only wrong if practiced in association with idolatry? Paul was saying that the mind that rebels against the knowledge of God will naturally rebel against the laws of God, including those laws prohibiting
homosexuality.

The homosexual advocate must engage in interpretive gymnastics
to neutralize the clear teaching in Scripture regarding homosexuality.
Frankly, it would be more intellectually honest to simply dismiss the
Bible rather than twisting its meaning into such tortured explanations.
As I noted earlier, a rule for interpretation we would all do well to fol-
low says, "When plain sense makes good sense, seek no other sense."

Myth four: "Science has proved that people are born gay." Citing three
well-known (but, as we will see, highly flawed) studies "proving" a genetic
link to homosexuality, homosexual advocates argue, "If God created
people to be homosexual, why would He condemn them for it?" The
question requires both a biological and a theological response.

Let's first examine this myth from a biological standpoint. Has
science confirmed that people are born gay? Many homosexual proponents point to three studies that "prove" that homosexuality is an inherited tendency: First, they cite the hypothalamus study conducted by
Dr. Simon LeVay in 1991. Dr. LeVay dissected the brains of thirty-five
male corpses, including nineteen professed homosexuals who had died
of AIDS, and he discovered that a portion of the hypothalamus in the
brains of the homosexual men was smaller than in those of the heterosexual men.[11] However, there were several glaring problems with the
study. First, six of the sixteen "heterosexual" brains in the study came

from men who had also died of AIDS, calling into question whether they were truly heterosexual.[12]

Second, if one accepts Dr. LeVay's assertions concerning a difference in the brain size of homosexuals and heterosexuals, one has to ask whether that variation is the *cause* of homosexual activity or the *result* of homosexual activity. It is also possible that AIDS could be responsible for the difference.[13]

Third, Dr. LeVay's study has never been replicated, which, as any scientist knows, is essential to confirming a theory.[14] So seriously flawed is LeVay's work that Dr. Anne Fausto-Sterling of Brown University said, "My freshman biology students know enough to sink this study."[15] It should also be noted that Dr. LeVay approached this study with a definite agenda. After the death of his own lover, Dr. LeVay told *Newsweek* magazine that he was determined to find a genetic cause for homosexuality or he would give up science completely. LeVay was determined to change legal and religious attitudes toward homosexuals by proving a genetic link.[16] While Dr. LeVay's sexual preferences and social agenda do not automatically discredit his "findings," one must question his objectivity.

A second widely reported study indicating a genetic link to homosexuality was the Bailey and Pillard study of twins. A sampling of 110 homosexual men who were identical or fraternal twins revealed that 52 percent of those who were identical twins had brothers who were also homosexual, while only 22 percent of the men who were fraternal (nonidentical) twins had homosexual brothers. Among nontwin brothers, the study showed the rate of homosexuality to be 9.2 percent.[17] On the surface, the much higher incidence of homosexuality among identical twins seems to indicate that there must be some biological cause.[18]

But like the LeVay study, this project was also defective. First, the representatives in the sample were recruited through solicitations in homosexual publications and organizations, causing doubts about how representative these samples were.[19] Second, one must consider the 48 percent statistic indicating that homosexual men had identical twins who were *not* homosexual.[20] Doesn't the fact that nearly half of the sample were not gay indicate that something other than genetics alone causes homosexuality? Third, all of the twins in the study were reared in the same households.[21] Had they lived in separate homes, it would be easier to believe that nature rather than nurture was responsible for their sexual orientation. Furthermore, the fact that twice as many fraternal twins (22 percent) as nontwin siblings (9.2 percent) were homosexual is hard to understand since fraternal twins do not share any more genetic traits than nontwin siblings. This raises further suspicion about how representative these sample families were.[22]

The third study that supposedly proves a biological causation for homosexuality involves the discovery of "the gay gene." In July 1993 *Science* magazine reported that Dr. Dean Hamer had discovered genetic markers on the X chromosome of thirty-three out of forty nonidentical homosexual twin brothers, "proving" a genetic link to homosexuality.[23]

However, there are several problems with this study as well. First, the study has not been replicated, which in scientific jargon means that it has not yet been verified.[24] Also, the presence of such a marker does not automatically prove causation. For example, this gene might cause twin brothers to be more inclined to identify with each other or to be attracted to novel or dangerous behavior, or to have any number of inclinations other than homosexual tendencies.[25]

In 1993 William Byne and Bruce Parsons, researchers at the New York State Psychiatric Institute, reviewed all the evidence for the theory of biological causation of homosexuality presented by Dr. LeVay and

Drs. Bailey and Pillard. They concluded in the *Archives of General Psychiatry* that "there is no evidence at the present to substantiate a biologic theory [of sexual orientation]."[26] But what if at some future date incontrovertible evidence is discovered proving that homosexuality is an inherited tendency?

That leads us to the theological response to this myth. Proving that homosexuality is result of genetics does not automatically legitimize homosexual behavior. Recent studies indicate that a number of behaviors such as alcoholism, violence, and adultery may have genetic roots. Yet are we willing to excuse such behavior by saying, "My genes made me do it"? The truth is that *all* tendencies toward sin are inherited. Our forefather Adam passed down to each one of us an innate desire to rebel against God's laws: "Therefore, just as through one man sin entered into the world, and death through sin, and so death spread to all men, because all sinned" (Romans 5:12).

That magnetic pull toward the forbidden, present in all of our hearts, manifests itself in different ways. Some are drawn toward adultery, some toward violence, some toward substance abuse, and some (possibly) toward homosexuality. Whether those desires are caused by nature (biological factors), by nurture (environmental factors), or by some combination of both is ultimately inconsequential. None of us gets a "pass" from God for rebellious behavior just because it arises from our innate desires, regardless of the cause of those desires. But here is the good news: Through the power of Jesus Christ, all of us can be freed from acting on those desires.

Myth five: "Homosexuals enjoy the same kinds of healthy, monogamous relationships as heterosexuals." If you are a regular viewer of the cable news programs on television, you have probably seen a heated debate concerning the right of gay couples to adopt children. People such as former talk-show host Rosie O'Donnell and other famous gay activists ask, "What's wrong with a child living in a home where two people who just happen to be homosexual love each other? Isn't that better than living in a home where a man and woman are constantly fighting with each other?" Whether on news programs or in fictional series, most gay couples on television are portrayed as being in long-term, monogamous relationships.

But such relationships are a myth in the real world. Dr. J. McIlhaney of the Medical Institute for Sexual Health reports that only 10 percent of male homosexuals and 25 percent of female homosexuals could be described as being "close-coupled," a term that means they have a lower number of recent sexual partners and less propensity to "cruise" than the average homosexual—an average which is incredibly higher than among the heterosexual population.[27]

For example, according to the most widely accepted study by Bell and Weinburg (1978) on the subject, 43 percent of the male homosexuals in San Francisco estimated that they had had sexual encounters with more than 500 men. Twenty-eight percent had engaged in sex with more than 1,000 men![28] In another study of 655 San Francisco gays conducted in 1985, only 24 percent had been monogamous during that past year.[29] According to one study, gays average somewhere between 106 and 1,105 partners a year.[30]

And what kind of sexual behavior do they engage in? If you are squeamish, you might want to skip this paragraph. Homosexuals do not simply hold hands, kiss, or even engage in a simulation of heterosexual intimacy. Instead, studies show that almost all homosexuals engage in oral sex, 90 percent have engaged in anal sex, many practice fisting (inserting one's fist into the partner's rectum), about 80 percent participate in fecal sex (licking and/or inserting their tongues into the anus of their partners and ingesting medically significant amounts of feces), and between 10 and 30 percent of gays participate in "golden showers" (drinking or being splashed with their partner's urine).[31]

Such perversions explain the significantly higher incidence of hepatitis, syphilis, and AIDS among gays. And by the way, don't allow anyone to mislead you concerning AIDS: It is primarily a homosexual disease that results from homosexual behavior. "In 1998 alone, 16,642 AIDS cases were reported among homosexual men, whereas only 6,735 AIDS cases were reported among heterosexual men and women combined"[32] (and quite possibly a number of them were actually bisexual). Homosexual men are eight times more likely to contract hepatitis, fourteen times more likely to contract syphilis.[33] "Homosexuals account for 80% of the serious sexually transmitted diseases in the United States."[34]

The destructive nature of homosexuality manifests itself in other ways as well. One study has demonstrated that between 25 and 33 percent of homosexual men and women are alcoholics,[35] and gay men are 6 times more likely to attempt suicide than heterosexual men.[36] Homosexuals are 18 times more likely to be involved in fatal traffic accidents and 116 times more likely to be murdered than heterosexuals. Death from murder, suicide, or accidents among homosexual women in the 25–44 age bracket is 487 times higher than heterosexual Caucasian women of the same age.[37]

These statistics prove that homosexual relationships are neither "normal" nor "healthy."

Myth six: "Ten percent of the population is homosexual." You have probably heard this statistic cited often, and yet there is absolutely no basis for it. Where did this "10-percent" figure originate? More than fifty years ago, Dr. Alfred Kinsey released a study titled *Sexual Behavior in the Human Male* in which he claimed that 10 percent of the 5,300 men he surveyed claimed to have been homosexual for three years.[38] But there are several problems with extrapolating from this study that 10 percent of the entire population is homosexual.

First, these 10 percent had not necessarily been homosexual all of their lives, nor did they necessarily retain a homosexual orientation for the remainder of their lives. As we will see in the next section, one's sexual orientation is not as fixed as we are led to believe. Also, the sample Kinsey used for his study could hardly be called representative of the population. Twenty-five percent of the men surveyed were prisoners, a group from which you would naturally expect a higher incidence of homosexuality.[39]

More recent studies have discredited the 10-percent myth. A survey of 3,321 men in 1993 revealed that only 2.3 percent of them had engaged in any kind of homosexual conduct within the last ten years, and only 1.1 percent claimed to be exclusively homosexual.[40]

Indeed, even some homosexual activists know that the 10-percent estimate is absurdly high, but they continue to propagate the myth. One advocate confesses, "I think people probably always did know that it [the 10-percent figure] was inflated, but it was a nice number that you could point to...that you could say, 'one-in-ten' and it's a fairly good way to get people to visualize that we are here."[41]

Why are homosexual activists intent on perpetuating the 10-percent myth? First, the inflated number is a way to "normalize" homosexuality. How can one argue that homosexuality is abnormal if so many people are gay? This line of reasoning is obviously deficient. Even if one accepts the highly doubtful 10-percent figure, does that automatically make homosexuality acceptable? Studies have shown that between 10 and 15 percent of the Americans are alcoholics, but does anyone really want to argue that alcoholism is desirable or normal?

But there is a more insidious reason behind this propaganda. By inflating the percentage, homosexual apologists are able to cover over the darkest secret associated with this perversion: child molestation. To those who try to establish a link between pedophilia (sex with children) and homosexuality, the homosexual advocate will point out that "only" 20 to 40 percent of child molestations are committed by homosexuals. That is true. However, since homosexuals represent such a small part of the population, that means they are responsible for a disproportionate number of sexual assaults against children.

For example, if 2 percent of the population is homosexual and these people are responsible for 20 to 40 percent of child molestations, that means a child is ten to twenty times more likely to be assaulted by a homosexual than by a heterosexual. Obviously, the higher the percentage of the population that is homosexual, the lower the differential between homosexual and heterosexual child molesters. Yet even if one accepts the 10-percent myth, a child is still two to four times more likely to be molested by a homosexual than by a heterosexual.

Amazingly, many gay activists do not attempt to hide the link between homosexuality and pedophilia. They are actively involved in legalizing sex between adults and children. In an article titled "Pedophilia and the Gay Movement," published in the *Journal of Homosexuality*, author Theo Sandfort chronicles efforts to end "the oppression towards pedophilia." He notes that in 1980 the largest Dutch gay organization (the COC) "adopted the position that the liberation of pedophilia must be viewed as a gay issue...[and that] ages of consent should therefore be abolished.... By acknowledging the affinity between homosexuality and pedophilia, the COC has quite possibly made it easier for homosexual adults to become more sensitive to erotic desires of younger members of their sex, thereby broadening gay identity."[42]

Ten years later the COC succeeded in lowering the age of consent for homosexual sex to twelve (unless parents object, in which case it is raised to fifteen).[43] In Hawaii, activists attempted to lower the consent age to fourteen, and their efforts continue unabated. In the Washington March for Gay Pride in 1993, activists chanted, "We're here. We're queer. And we're coming after your children."

Myth seven: "Homosexuality is a fixed desire and cannot be changed." According to this commonly held belief, since homosexuals are born with a biological and therefore immutable homosexual orientation, any attempt to persuade them to change is both cruel and futile. Yet, as we have already demonstrated, the link between genetics and homosexuality is dubious at best. But the other part of the assumption is equally fallacious. A person's sexual preferences are much more fluid than homosexual advocates would want you to know. A study released by the Kinsey Report in 1970 revealed that:

- Eighty-one percent of gays and 93 percent of lesbians had changed or shifted their sexual behavior after age twelve.
- Fifty-eight percent of gays and 77 percent of lesbians reported a second shift in sexual preferences.
- Thirty-one percent of gays and 49 percent of lesbians reported a third shift.
- Thirteen percent of gays and 30 percent of lesbians reported a fourth shift before they engaged in homosexual conduct exclusively.
- Twenty-nine percent of heterosexual men and 14 percent of heterosexual women reported at least one shift in sexual orientation.
- Seventy-four percent of homosexual men have been sexually aroused by a female, and eighty percent of lesbians reported having been sexually aroused by a male.[44]

Dr. Irving Bieber, director of the New York Center for Psycho-analytic Training, has treated more than one hundred homosexuals who desired to change their sexual orientation. His conclusion? "A hetero-sexual shift is a possibility for all homosexuals who are strongly moti-vated to change."[45] Furthermore, the misinformation that homosexual-ity is fixed and therefore unchangeable results in "incalculable harm to thousands."[46]

When I brought up the issue of choice to the girl I was counseling, Susan responded, "Robert, do you think I would *choose* to engage in this lifestyle that is filled with deception, loneliness, and danger? I would give anything if I could change." Yet the myth of immutability as well as the other six myths that she had embraced were about to sentence her to an existence plagued by physical disease, emotional disorder, and spiritual distance from God.

I wish I could report that after hearing the above information, she renounced her homosexual tendencies, confessed her sin to God, and left my office with a newfound attraction to the opposite sex. She didn't. But she did promise to consider the most important question for a Christian who engages in homosexual conduct: "What does God *really* think about my behavior? Am I interpreting the Bible through the lens of my homosexuality, or am I interpreting my homosexuality through the lens of Scripture?"

For a Christian, an honest answer to that question is the starting place for genuine healing and lasting change.

Husbands Are to Be the Leaders of Their Families

A few years ago I was performing a wedding ceremony for some members of a church I formerly pastored. After reading from 1 Corinthians 13 about the supremacy of love and from Ephesians 5 about the roles and responsibilities in marriage, it was time to get down to the business of the vows. First, I asked the bride, "Do you, Sara, take Bill to be your lawful and wedded husband? Do you promise to love and obey him until death alone shall part you?"

She answered, "Yes."

I then asked Bill if he promised to love Sara with the same unconditional love with which Christ loved us, to the point of laying down his life for his wife. After mulling the question over for a few minutes (just kidding), Bill enthusiastically answered, "Yes."

After the service a sweet-looking little old lady (is there any other kind?) approached me and introduced herself as the bride's grandmother. Suddenly her countenance was transformed as she said, "Reverend, if you had asked *me* the same question you asked my granddaughter about obeying her husband, I would have answered, 'Hell, no!'" With that she stomped off to the reception for some punch and cookies.

Her reaction is not that unusual. In 1998 the Southern Baptist Convention created a maelstrom of controversy (something we are rather gifted at doing) by issuing a proclamation about the family that said, in part, that a wife is to "submit graciously to the servant leadership of her husband." After that pronouncement, a 1998 Gallup Poll revealed that 69 percent of the respondents disagreed with that statement. A few days after the Baptists issued their report, I saw a cartoon in *Newsweek* depicting a cave man holding a club in one hand and dragging his wife by the hair with the other hand. An onlooker commented to his friend, "Must be a Southern Baptist."

Indeed, even to many evangelical Christians, the idea of wives' submitting to their husbands seems antiquated or even misogynistic. More than ten years ago, *Christianity Today* surveyed its predominantly evangelical subscribers regarding the issue of male headship in the family. About 90 percent of males and females combined agreed with the statement "The Bible affirms the principle of male headship in the family." Yet the understanding of "headship" varied greatly among the respondents. Slightly more than one-third of male and female respondents seemed to disagree with the statement that "the husband holds ultimate responsibility for all major decisions in the family and the home."[1]

More than a decade later, the magazine again polled its readership and discovered that there is a great deal of confusion among Christians regarding the roles of males and females. In fact, only 19 percent of the respondents believed that the Bible's teachings on the subject are "very clear and plainly understood." That figure explains why 78 percent of those surveyed believe that "Christian leaders need to speak out on proper roles for men and women."[2]

And yet when they *do* speak out, they are criticized for promoting a hierarchical view of marriage from the Dark Ages that leads to the oppression and abuse of women—a very present reality for many women living in the twenty-first century.

I pastor a conservative Southern Baptist church in which women would never be permitted to serve as deacons or pastors. Yet whenever I teach from such passages as Ephesians 5 in which Paul instructed wives to submit to their husbands because "the husband is the head of the wife" (verse 23), you can cut the tension in the congregational atmosphere with a knife. In many minds, Paul's status immediately changes from "God's chosen apostle" to "male chauvinist pig."

Why do so many women and men react negatively to the concept that wives are to submit to their husbands? Some would respond that all of us have a natural tendency to oppose any God-ordained theology. Others would point to cultural changes, such as women working outside the home or serving in the armed forces, that make submission appear outdated. Still others would lament the inroads that the feminist movement has made in the thinking of Christians and non-Christians alike.

While all of these reasons have some validity, I would like to suggest another reason many react so viscerally to the idea of submission. I believe some Christian leaders, in an attempt to clarify the biblical teachings about the roles of men and women in marriage, have twisted Paul's words about submission to say something the apostle never intended to communicate.

In this chapter I want to rescue the biblical teaching on submission from the radical feminists, as well as from the rabid fundamentalists, and discover what the Bible *really* teaches about a wife's responsibility to her husband and a husband's responsibility to his wife.

The seminal passage in the Bible that explains submission is the one I alluded to in the wedding ceremony. It's the passage that sent Grandma's blood pressure soaring. Yet when we look at Paul's words in context, they do not seem nearly as chauvinistic as you might be led to believe.

In Ephesians 5 Paul explains how our relationship to Christ should impact our family life. Specifically, Paul was dealing with the three most common relationships in the typical Greco-Roman household: husbands and wives; parents and children; and slaves and masters (slaves lived in the home in those days). Understandably, Paul began with the foundational relationship of a husband and wife:

> Wives, be subject to your own husbands, as to the Lord. For the husband is the head of the wife, as Christ also is the head of the church, He Himself being the Savior of the body. But as the church is subject to Christ, so also the wives ought to be to their husbands in everything. Husbands, love your wives, just as Christ also loved the church and gave Himself up for her.... So husbands ought also to love their own wives as their own bodies. (verses 22-25,28)

This central passage on the responsibilities of husbands and wives in marriage reveals six principles about the highly charged and often misunderstood subject of subjection, or submission, as we will call it.

1. "Submission is mutual." Submission in marriage has become a battleground in many denominations and in many marriages, with neither side of the debate willing to yield an inch of territory. One side (egalitarians) argues that men and women are equal in God's eyes and therefore have both the capacity and the right to be joint decision makers in marriage. While some opponents of submission easily dismiss the

Ephesians 5 passage as irrelevant in today's culture, there are a number of Christians from the egalitarian camp who accept this passage of Scripture as God's authoritative message for today.

So how do they handle the clear command in verse 22 for wives to "be subject to your own husbands"? They quickly point to the preceding verse that commands all Christians to "be subject to one another in the fear of Christ" (verse 21). "Yes, wives are to submit to their husbands," they concede, "but husbands are *also* to submit to their wives. Paul was teaching 'mutual submission.'"

Those who advocate a complementarian view of marriage—the belief that while husbands and wives are equal before God, they have different God-assigned roles in marriage—balk at the idea of mutual submission. "There has to be a chain of command in any organization; otherwise there will be chaos. If you advocate mutual submission in marriage, then you have to believe in mutual submission between parents and children, which Paul discusses in the next section. Who in their right mind would argue that parents should obey their children in the same way children are commanded to obey their parents?" Good point, you must admit.

So which camp is right? Both are—to an extent. The egalitarians are correct in pointing out that this passage begins with a call for all Christians to "be subject to one another" (verse 21). The word translated "be subject to" is a military term that means "to arrange or rank under." As Christians we are to place ourselves "under" one another, meaning that we are to put other Christians' interests ahead of our own. I remember hearing Dr. Howard Hendricks tell a story of two rams who met each other on a narrow mountain pass. There was not room enough for both to continue, so they spent a considerable amount of time butting heads as each one tried to seize the advantage. Eventually, one of the rams realized they were at an impasse and chose to kneel, allowing the other ram to climb over him. His voluntary submission resulted in mutual benefits since each ram could then continue his journey.

Jesus Christ exemplified this kind of submission when He willingly gave up all the privileges of heaven to descend to earth and die for our sins. Just as Jesus placed our needs above His rights, Paul encourages us to emulate that same attitude in our families.

So how does this principle actually work in our homes? Wives are to put their husband's needs above their own, just as husbands are to elevate their wife's needs above their own desires. The same reciprocal truth applies to parents and children as well as to masters and slaves. Mutual submission of our rights is the lubricant that ensures a smooth-running home.

But mutual submission does not strip a husband of his responsibility and authority to lead his family. While complementarians (those who teach that husbands are responsible for decision making) are wrong for ignoring the clear call for mutual submission in verse 21, egalitarians (those who advocate equal authority between husbands and wives) are so focused on verse 21 that they miss the rest of the passage that highlights the differences between husbands and wives.

A wife submits to her husband by following his leadership as the "head" of the family (a term we will examine later). A husband submits to his wife by placing her needs above his own. The husband is to surrender his rights, but never his responsibility to lead.

Author Wayne Grudem illustrated the difference between surrendering our rights and surrendering our responsibility. Dr. Grudem was a well-respected New Testament scholar at Trinity International University in Deerfield, Illinois. His wife, Margaret, had suffered for several years from constant pain due to fibromyalgia. The Grudems noticed that Margaret's pain subsided whenever they visited the hot, arid climate of Arizona. They began to talk about moving to Arizona so that Margaret could find relief from her discomfort. Yet such a move would certainly hinder Dr. Grudem's career since he would be forced to give up his post at a prestigious university and move to a lesser-known school.

"I came to Ephesians 5:28, 'Even so husbands should love their wives as their own bodies,' " he later wrote. "If I were to love my own wife as I love my own body, then shouldn't I move [to Arizona] for the sake of Margaret?" How does Dr. Grudem's view differ from the egalitarian view that neither the husband nor the wife has the final say in decisions? Grudem continued, "Our decision process did not look at all like mutual submission.... I did decide to move to Arizona out of love for my wife, and I believe the Bible teaches a lot of mutual things, like mutual love and mutual deference to each other's needs, preferences, and desires. But at no time did I submit to Margaret's authority or yield my leadership role in the marriage."[3]

2. *"Submission is based on assigned roles, not on inherent worth."* My brother is a police lieutenant in Dallas, Texas. During the years he has spent on the beat, he has often had to turn on his lights, activate his siren, pull traffic violators off to the side of the road, and issue tickets. What motivates a driver to "submit" to my brother? In some instances, the driver might be more intelligent, wealthier, or even more spiritual than my brother, but that is not the issue, is it? My brother has been given an assigned role (and the corresponding authority) by the government to enforce the law.

Similarly, the reason wives are commanded to submit to their husbands has nothing to do with inherent worth, but rather with assigned responsibility. Nowhere does the Bible perpetrate the idea that women are inferior to men. Instead, the Bible consistently elevates the status of women.

I remember one of my seminary professors claiming that Paul's words about the role of women could not be accepted as authoritative because Paul was "a bitter, old bachelor who hated women." Yet the fact that Paul began his discussion about home life by addressing the women in the Ephesian congregation demonstrates a level of respect for women absent in Paul's culture.

The Romans viewed women as chattel and saw marriage as little more than legalized prostitution. In the Jewish world, many men began the morning by praying, "God, I thank you that I am not a Gentile, a slave, or a woman." As for the enlightened Greeks, the renowned philosopher Aristotle summed up their view of the female species: "The female is female by virtue of a lack of certain qualities. We should regard the female in nature as afflicted with natural defectiveness."[4]

Contrast that kind of thinking with the biblical view, which elevated rather than denigrated women. Jesus Christ shocked the Samaritan woman at the well by taking time to converse with her (see John 4). No respectable rabbi would ever hold a theological discussion with a woman. Or consider Peter's admonition to husbands to grant their wives "honor as a fellow heir of the grace of life" (1 Peter 3:7). Paul clearly affirmed the equality of women with men when he wrote, "There is neither Jew nor Greek, there is neither slave nor free man, there is neither male nor female; for you are all one in Christ Jesus" (Galatians 3:28). Hardly sounds like the musings of a bitter, old bachelor who hates women.

But equality does not mean "sameness." For example, is red equal to blue? Well, they are both colors, but they are not the same colors. Is hot better than cold? No, they are both temperatures, but one is better suited for coffee and the other for ice cream.

Similarly, men and women are equal in their status before God, but they are also different. For example, consider just a few of the numerous physiological differences between the sexes:

- On average, men are taller and weigh more than women. (Compared with an eighteen-year-old woman, an eighteen-year-old man is, on average, 5.8 inches taller and 18.2 pounds heavier.)
- Men have 50 percent more muscle mass per pound than women, making women only 80 percent as strong as males of approximately the same size.
- Women have 10 percent more body fat than men of the same age. Women tend to accumulate fat in the buttocks, thighs, and arms, while men accumulate fat in the abdomen, chest, and back.
- The pelvic structure of women is wider than men, and they have less bone mass. This difference makes men more efficient runners.
- On average, a woman's heart is 25 percent smaller than a man's. Consequently, men's hearts pump more blood per beat, and their resting heart rates are as much as five to eight beats slower than women's resting heart rates.
- Women have a smaller lung capacity than men. On average, men have a 25 to 30 percent greater lung capacity than women, making them more efficient in aerobic activities such as running.[5]

Equality does not mean sameness. God created men and women differently so they would be equipped to fulfill their unique purposes.

3. "Submission is part of God's created order." One question I am continually asked is, Why would God place a man who is intellectually, emotionally, and even spiritually inferior to his wife in authority over her? It's one thing to submit to someone who is recognizably superior to you, but how do you submit to someone who is demonstrably inferior to you? Duane Litfin offers some helpful insight here:

It may never be understood why God gives a husband who is inferior to his wife a position of authority over her, any more than one can explain why God gives civil officials who are inferior to most of the populace a position of authority over them. In both cases the Christian's responsibility is to submit "as to the Lord" to those whom God has placed in authority, recognizing that such submission is not because the individual holding the position of authority is necessarily a superior human being, but rather because respect is due to the sovereign wisdom of the God who ordained that relationship of authority and submission. (Rom. 13:1-2)[6]

Paul tells us that according to God's organizational chart for marriage, the husband "is the head of the wife, as Christ also is the head of the church" (Ephesians 5:23). He doesn't qualify the statement by saying "some husbands are the head of some wives" or "the husband—if he is spiritually and intellectually qualified—is the head of the wife." No, God desires that every husband serve as the head of every marriage relationship.

In recent years there has been a fierce debate over the meaning of the word translated "head" (*kephale* in Greek). When we think of someone as the "head" over something or someone else, we picture that person as the one who gives direction, just as our head gives direction to other parts of our body. How do egalitarians, who reject the idea of husbands' being in authority over their wives, get around this verse that declares the husband to be "the head of the wife"? They claim that the Greek word *kephale* means "source" rather than "authority."

New Testament scholars who, like Dr. Wayne Grudem, reject the egalitarian point of view and advocate a husband's authority over the wife respond by demonstrating that the word *kephale* clearly means "authority." Dr. Grudem found that of 2,336 instances in ancient Greek literature in which the word *kephale* was used, it never meant "source."[7] In forty-nine instances, *kephale* clearly had the meaning of "person of superior authority or rank,"[8] making "head" an acceptable translation of the word, especially given the context of its usage in the New Testament.

To support the idea that the word *kephale* means "source" or "origin," opponents will point to biblical and extrabiblical uses of the word such as in Colossians 1:18, which refers to Christ as the "head of the body, the church." Did Paul mean that Christ is in authority over the church or that He is the origin or life-giving source of the church? One could easily argue both. Certainly, it is Jesus Christ who infuses the church with life, but it is equally obvious that He is also the supreme authority over the church.

Frankly, this whole linguistic argument over the meaning of *kephale* misses the bigger point. From the very beginning, God created the husband to be in authority over his wife. After God created the world, the animals, and finally Adam, He observed, "It is not good for the man to be alone; I will make him a *helper* suitable for him" (Genesis 2:18).

Notice that Adam was created to rule over the earth, cultivate the ground, and name the animals. But God gave the woman the role of being Adam's helper. The Hebrew word translated "helper" means "to give assistance to." The primary reason the first woman was created was to assist her husband in his God-given assignment.

Ladies, before you slam this book shut in disgust and throw it at something (or someone), let me quickly point out that your designation as your husband's helper in no way infers that you are inferior to him. This word *helper* is used twenty-one times in the Old Testament. Interestingly, fifteen of those times the word is used to describe God. The

Lord is described as humankind's helper, ready to make up for our weaknesses.

Similarly, God designed women to be a helper for men to compensate for our deficiencies (such as always leaving the toilet seat up). The Bible teaches that men are just as helpless without women as they are without God. That is why I laughed aloud when I read these testosterone-charged words from a popular Christian book that encourages men to reclaim their manhood: "A man does not go to a woman to get his strength; he goes to her to *offer* it. You do not need the woman for you to become a great man, and as a great man you do not need the woman."[9]

The author sounds macho, but he is sadly mistaken. Men, we *do* need women to be complete. Unless God has called you to be single, you are deficient without a woman in your life. That is why God says, "I will make him a helper suitable for him."

Also included in God's original plan was the husband's authority over his wife. For example, Genesis 5:2 tells us that God gave Eve the same name He had given her husband Adam, not vice versa. The practice in Western culture of a wife's assuming her husband's name is not some quaint but outdated custom from the Victorian era. This is one way God has demonstrated headship in marriage.[10]

The fact that God's original plan for marriage included the headship of the husband is also seen in the way God dealt with Adam and Eve's sin. Although Adam and Eve were both guilty of violating God's command, God first spoke with Adam about the couple's disobedience. Why? Because God had installed Adam as the leader in his family, and with that role came responsibility.

Some egalitarians will grudgingly concede that the husband is in authority over the wife, but they point out that such an arrangement was never part of God's original plan; instead, they argue, it was the result of the first couple's fall into sin. As evidence of their view, they cite the curse placed on Eve (and all women) as a result of her disobedience:

> To the woman He said,
> "I will greatly multiply
> Your pain in childbirth,
> In pain you will bring forth children;
> Yet your desire will be for your husband,
> And he will rule over you." (Genesis 3:16)

As a result of the Fall, God's original plan for equality in marriage was replaced by authoritarianism in which the man "rules" over the wife, or so the theory goes. But let's look further at the last part of Genesis 3:16. What does God mean when He says that from this point on Eve's desire would be for her husband? Is sexual desire part of God's judgment? Hardly! As I recall, Adam and Eve were getting along pretty well in the prefig-leaf days! Sex was always part of God's plan. The word translated "desire" means "to take control" or "to usurp." Part of the fallout from the first couple's sin would be that women would attempt to usurp their husband's leadership in the home.

And how would husbands respond? They would endeavor to "rule" over their wife. The word *rule* does not mean "to lead in a loving way." Instead, it means to dominate in an oppressive manner. The late James Montgomery Boice said that this verse marks the beginning of the battle of the sexes in which women would attempt to seize control of their homes, and husbands would overreact with authoritarian heavy-handedness.[11] We see that same struggle played out today in the homes of believers as well as unbelievers.

But through the power of Jesus Christ in our lives, we are released from that pattern of rebellion and authoritarianism so that we can rediscover God's original plan for marriage in which a wife willingly defers to her husband's leadership, and the husband sacrificially loves and leads his wife.

In every institution God has created—the government, the church, the workplace, or the home—He has also established a hierarchy to maintain order. As a friend of mine says, "Anything in nature with two heads is a freak, and anything with no head is dead!" That doesn't mean that a husband—or any other leader for that matter—should act unilaterally without seeking counsel. A wise husband will invite and listen to the advice of his wife since she is a "fellow heir in the grace of God," as Peter said. Frequently a wife can offer valuable insight into a situation. Pilate would have done himself a great service had he heeded his wife's counsel to leave Jesus Christ alone rather than cave in to the public's demand for blood.

Nevertheless, in any organization someone must have the final decision-making power, and according to God's design, that responsibility rests with the husband.

4. "Submission is voluntary." I love the story that Rabbi Harold Kushner tells about a conversation he had with a soon-to-be bride who said that she was planning on assuming her fiancé's last name once they were married. Kushner was surprised by her admission, knowing something of her beliefs about the roles of men and women.

"I had the impression you were a staunch feminist," Kushner remarked.

"I am," the young woman replied. "If I'm to be known by some guy's name, I'd rather it be the guy I chose than the guy my mother chose."[12] When I say that submission is voluntary, I do not mean that wives have the right to selectively follow their husband's leadership when it suits them. Instead, submission is voluntary in the sense that every woman chooses whether or not she wants to marry and, consequently, live under the authority of a husband.

Social psychologists have identified five types of power that human beings exercise over one another. When the authority figure is able to influence another person through the information he gives or withholds, he is using *information power.* When the authority figure motivates the subordinate to want to be like her through her positive example, she is using *referent power.* When the authority figure has the power to offer punishment or reward to a subordinate, he is exerting *coercive-reward power.* When the authority figure is more gifted or skilled than a subordinate, she possesses *expert power.* However, *positional power* describes a subordinate's decision to obey a superior solely because of the position that superior holds.

According to the New Testament, the only kind of power or authority a husband possesses over his wife is the positional power conferred on him by God. The other four kinds of power are equally available to both husbands and wives.[13] For example, we can all think of instances in which a wife exerts power over her husband through the information she possesses, by her behavior, by withholding or granting rewards, or by possessing superior skills (such as managing finances). But positional power is reserved for the husband alone and is the only one of the five kinds of power that has nothing to do with the inherent superiority of the one exercising it. The wife is to submit to her husband solely because of the position God has given to him. To paraphrase the old military cliché: "You salute the La-Z-Boy, not the man in the La-Z-Boy." Paul said it a little more eloquently, "Wives, be subject to your own husbands, as to the Lord" (Ephesians 5:22).

In marriage, two people who are equal in worth come together in a union in which the woman voluntarily places herself under the positional authority of her husband. The best illustration of such voluntary submission is found in the Godhead. Paul wrote, "But I want you to understand that Christ is the head of every man, and the man is the head of a woman, and God is the head of Christ" (1 Corinthians 11:3).

Think for a moment about the relationship between God the Father and Jesus Christ the Son. Are the Father and the Son equal? Of course They are! The essence of historic Christianity is the belief in the equality of all three Persons in the Godhead—Father, Son, and Holy Spirit. Yet even though Jesus was equal to God the Father, He willingly gave up His rights as the Father's equal, assumed the limitations of humanity, submitted His will to the Father's will, and became "obedient to the point of death, even death on a cross" (Philippians 2:8). God the Father did not demand that Jesus submit to Him. Christ willingly placed Himself under the authority of His Father.

In the same way, no one (at least in our culture) forces a woman to marry. She is free to remain single as long as she desires. But should she choose to enter a marriage relationship, she is voluntarily placing herself under her husband's leadership.

5. *"Submission is limited."* One of the most frequently voiced objections to submission is that it gives license to a husband's physical abuse of his wife. Such a concern is not without merit. In a survey of 5,700 pastors in the United States and Canada, clinical psychologist Jim Alsdurf discovered that

- Twenty-six percent of pastors polled routinely told women who were being abused to continue submitting to their husbands and have faith that God would either end the abuse or give them the strength to endure it.

- Twenty-five percent of pastors said that it was the wife's lack of submissiveness that caused the abuse and that the abuse would stop if the wife would "learn to submit."
- Fifty percent of pastors said that it would be better for women to tolerate a certain level of violence in the home rather than seek a divorce.
- Seventy-one percent of pastors said they would never counsel an abused wife to leave her husband or separate because of abuse, and 92 percent said they would never counsel her to divorce.[14]

No wonder abused women ranked pastors last on their list of people who could provide helpful counsel when they were facing abuse.[15]

Any discussion about a wife's submission to her husband must include an explanation about the boundaries of submission. First, submission is limited in its *sphere*. By that I mean that God never intended every woman in the world to submit to every man in the world. Single women are under no obligation to defer to their boyfriends except in the general sense that all Christians are to submit to one another. Nothing in the Bible prohibits a woman from leading a corporation, commanding a battalion of soldiers, or serving as president of the United States. The only two arenas in which a woman is to submit to male leadership are in the home and in the church (a subject beyond the scope of this chapter). But in every other relationship and structure, women are not obligated to submit to men solely because of gender.

Submission is also limited in *scope*. A wife once told me that her husband had asked her to participate in a three-way sexual encounter with another woman. Does submission require her to comply with her husband's request?

Often a woman will tell me that her non-Christian husband has forbidden her to attend church. Should she disobey God's command not to forsake "assembling together" with other believers (Hebrews 10:25)?

Does a wife's deference to her husband require her to endure physical abuse or to allow her husband to do the same or worse to her children?

Are there limits to submission?

I know, I know. Paul said that wives are to submit to their husbands "in everything." But the word *everything* must be balanced with the truth of Acts 5:29, which says, "We must obey God rather than men." Never is a wife obligated to do anything that violates the clear teaching of God's Word, such as engaging in immorality, forsaking worship with other believers, or allowing herself or her children to be physically abused.

Make no mistake about it. God hates violence as much as He hates immorality. In fact, the primary reason the Bible gives for the destruction of the world in the days of Noah was because "the earth was filled with violence" (Genesis 6:11). Our reverence for the sanctity of human life should be reserved not only for human beings inside the womb but for those outside the womb as well, including ourselves. One way we demonstrate our respect for human life is by protecting ourselves, as well as others, from those who would seek to injure or destroy God-given life.

Where is the line between submission to authority figures and obedience to God? Author John Stott explains it this way:

> If therefore they (husbands, pastors, parents, authority figures)
> misuse their God-given authority (e.g., by commanding what
> God forbids or forbidding what God commands), then our duty
> is no longer conscientiously to submit, but conscientiously to
> refuse to do so. For to submit in such circumstances would be to

disobey God. The principle is clear: we must submit right up to the point where obedience to human authority would involve disobedience to God.[16]

Many of the "But what if my husband…" objections to submission are removed when we understand that submission is limited both in its sphere and its scope.

6. *"Submission is encouraged by example, not coercion."* As I write these words, our church is involved in a project to raise more than twenty million dollars for a new worship center. For years our leaders carefully studied the needs of our church and concluded that this is God's will for our congregation. Although the vast majority has been supportive of the effort, a few people questioned the need and even my motive for this project. It seemed the harder other leaders and I pushed, the more resistant these vocal few became.

A few weeks before the leaders presented the project to our congregation for a vote, our family went out of town for a few days to enjoy some rest. While I was driving, God began to speak to me (this is not a phrase I use lightly) about the kind of gift I should give to the project. Trust me, the figure He gave me was so ridiculously high that I nearly drove off the road. But the more I listened, the more I realized that this was God's will for my life.

The following week I began to share with our congregation what God had said to me about the kind of sacrifice He had asked me to make (and yes, I did confer with my wife before arriving at a final decision). Then I said to the congregation, "I can't tell you what to give. All I can do is ask you to be open to what God might say to you." Instantly the attitude of that small group of opponents began to change, and their objections began to melt away. Why? Because when they saw my willingness to submit to God's leadership and sacrifice a large portion of my own net worth, they were encouraged to do the same.

That principle applies in the marriage relationship as well. Husbands, please listen to me: You can never effectively coerce your wife to obey you. Even if through manipulation or abuse you can force her to comply with your requests, you might have the same experience as the father who told his son to sit in the corner and then heard the child mutter, "I may be sitting on the outside, but I'm standing on the inside."

One writer describes a woman's experience visiting a Christian couple and watching "submission" in action. The woman noticed that the wife, Sheila, only spoke when her husband, Joe, gave permission either verbally or by some sign such as nodding his head. "What's going on?" the woman asked.

Joe replied, "We've discovered what headship really means, and how Sheila must show she is a submissive wife in every way. So I decided I must signal when she can speak. Also, Sheila has cut down almost all her church work so that she can devote herself entirely to being a real woman and wife."[17]

No wonder *submission* is such a dirty word to so many! The principle of headship and submission in marriage does not give the husband license to act like a little dictator, barking out orders such as "Do this," "Fix me that," or "Don't speak unless you're spoken to." In fact, it is significant that nowhere in the Bible does God command wives to "obey" their husbands. The word *obey* is used in the relationship between children and parents and between slaves and masters, but not between wives and husbands. A wife is never to be treated as a child or a slave, but as an equal partner in the marriage who submits to her husband's leadership, not because she is inferior, but because she voluntarily accepts God's design for marriage.

Husbands, although you cannot force your wife to submit to your leadership, you can encourage her submission the same way I encouraged my church's submission: by example and sacrifice. Has it ever occurred to you that one reason your wife may have difficulty placing herself under your authority is because she has never seen *you* submit to God's authority? There *is* a relationship between the two. Remember 1 Corinthians 11:3: "But I want you to understand that Christ is the head of every man, and the man is the head of a woman, and God is the head of Christ."

Before your wife feels comfortable following your leadership concerning her children, her finances, or her future, she needs the assurance that you are listening to God and have placed yourself under His authority. According to Paul, submission begins with the husband, not with the wife. Submission is an attitude that is better caught than taught.

Submission is encouraged not only by a husband's example but by his sacrifice as well. It is no accident that Paul spent twice as much time addressing the husband's responsibility to love and sacrifice for his wife as he did exhorting women to submit to their husbands. But have you noticed how little attention is given to that command?

> Husbands, love your wives, just as Christ also loved the church
> and gave Himself up for her.... So husbands ought also to love
> their own wives as their own bodies. He who love his own wife
> loves himself; for no one ever hated his own flesh, but nourishes
> and cherishes it, just as Christ also does the church. (Ephesians
> 5:25,28-29)

The fact that Paul would make any demands of husbands was a revolutionary concept in the apostle's day. In Greek culture a husband had no obligations whatsoever. He was free to come and go as he desired. But in God's design for marriage, a wife demonstrates her submission to her husband by deferring to his leadership, and a husband submits to his wife by placing her needs above his own. That's how mutual submission works in marriage.

Steve Farrar recounts a true story from the career of military leader Norman Schwarzkopf during the 1991 Persian Gulf War. Some of the companies in Schwarzkopf's battalion were suffering from low morale, so the general decided on Christmas Day to throw a feast for all the different companies in the battalion. Schwarzkopf carefully mapped out his plan to arise early in the morning and fly to each company, deliver the feast to the men, shake their hands, and thank them for their service.

When Schwarzkopf arrived at Company D, the men were overwhelmed that he would make such an effort on their behalf. The general casually inquired where the company commander was. He was told that the commander had gone back to headquarters to visit some of his men who were in the hospital.

After a grueling day, Schwarzkopf returned to headquarters late that night and asked if anyone had seen the commander of Company D. They reported that he had visited some of his men in the hospital and then had hung out in the company mess for a few hours, enjoying his Christmas dinner.

Schwarzkopf found him and asked the commander why he had not returned to his company when he had finished visiting the hospital. "Well, I wanted to enjoy some Christmas dinner, and then as long as I was here, I wanted to shower and put on some clean clothes," the commander responded.

"What about your troops?" Schwarzkopf asked. "Didn't you realize that it is your responsibility as leader to see that they are taken care of first? Don't you realize what you have communicated to them? If you're not willing to go through the discomfort of spending Christmas with them in the field, how do you expect them to believe you'll be with them in the heat of battle?"

The commander replied, "Frankly, sir, I don't like this company-command business. I don't like being responsible for the troops all the time. So sometimes I just take care of my needs."

Schwarzkopf immediately ordered him and another captain named Trujillo into a helicopter, and they returned to Company D. In front of the entire company of men who had assembled together, Schwarzkopf said to the negligent commander, "I am relieving you of your command of this company immediately because you don't care about your troops. You do not deserve to be a company commander in this battalion. Go over and get in the helicopter."

The general then turned to Captain Trujillo and said, "You are now in command.... Take care of these men." As General Schwarzkopf turned and walked to the helicopter, the men erupted in cheers.[18]

Husband, being the leader of your family is not a privilege to be exploited; it is a responsibility. You are to place the welfare of your wife above your own. If you are not willing to do that, then you have no more business getting married than does a woman who refuses to submit to the authority of her husband.

But if you do choose to marry, your Commander in Chief has issued you a direct order: "Husbands, love your wives, just as Christ also loved the church" (Ephesians 5:25). More often than not, you will discover that when you submit to God's leadership, your wife will gladly submit to yours.

CHAPTER Six

Evolution Is a Myth

On August 11, 1999, the Kansas State Board of Education made headlines around the world by daring to question the "fact" of evolution. The board (contrary to erroneous media reports) did not ban the teaching of evolution but simply deleted evolution from state assessment tests of student performance, since evolution was deemed to be an unproven theory. Proponents of evolution were outraged that anyone would dare to question the absolute certainty of their explanation for the origin of life. Robert Palazzo, an associate professor of molecular biosciences at the University of Kansas, signed a protest letter to the governor of Kansas claming that "the concept of evolution is inextricable from the language of all life sciences and is a cornerstone for learning by all those who seek an education in basic science, medicine, and ecology."[1]

Maxine Singer, president of the Carnegie Institution of Washington, wrote in an August 18, 1999, column in the *Washington Post* that omitting evolution from biology (which the Kansas board never proposed) "is comparable to leaving the U.S. Constitution out of civics lessons. Evolution is the framework that makes sense of the whole natural world."[2]

The strident defenders of evolution got their way. In 2001 a new board of education in Kansas reversed the previous decision, and evolution is once again presented in Kansas classrooms as a foundational fact of biology.

But is the case for evolution as solid as its advocates would have us believe?

Are the only people who question evolution Bible-thumping pinheads who refuse to acknowledge "facts" in order to hold on to the fable of Creation recorded in Genesis?

Why are proponents of evolution so reticent to allow other views of the origin of life to be presented in the classroom in spite of the fact that a Zogby poll taken in February 2000 revealed that "63.7% of those surveyed agreed that creationism needs to be part of the regular public school curriculum, including 38.9% who strongly agreed"?[3]

If this is true, why are evolutionists so adamant that this alternative explanation for life's origin never be mentioned in the classroom?

As we will discover in this chapter, evolution is more than a scientific theory; it is an alternative religious philosophy regarding the origin of life. In spite of a mountain of evidence against it, evolution's proponents are in the unenviable position of defending its absurd claims. Why? The alternative is to acknowledge the role of an outside Creator, and such an admission is unthinkable to the evolutionist.

Before we look at the compelling evidence against evolution, we need to understand what evolution is really all about.

WHAT IS EVOLUTION?

To keep from falling into the stereotype of the ignorant religious fanatic, we must clearly understand what the evolutionist claims about the origin of life. This introduction to PBS's award-winning television broadcast "The Miracle of Life" summarizes what the evolutionist believes about the beginning of life:

Four and a half billion years ago, the young planet Earth was a mass of cosmic dust or particles. It was almost completely engulfed by the shallow primordial seas. Powerful winds gathered random molecules from the atmosphere. Some were deposited in the seas. Tides and currents swept the molecules together. And somewhere in this ancient ocean the miracle of life began.... The first organized form of primitive life was a tiny protozoan [a one-celled animal]. Millions of protozoa populated the ancient seas. These early organisms were completely self-sufficient in their sea-water world. They moved about their aquatic environment feeding on bacteria and other organisms.... From these one-celled organisms evolved all life on earth.[4]

This prologue presents the three major tenets of evolution we need to comprehend before we can effectively combat it. First, *evolution seeks to explain the process, not the timetable, for the origin of life.* Evolution is not about time; it is about a process. Don't misunderstand. The evolutionist has some definite ideas about the age of the earth. She believes that the earth is about 4.5 billion years of age and that about 3.7 billion years ago a single-cell protozoan emerged from some primordial chemical soup. Billions of years are necessary in the evolutionist's scheme to allow for the multitude of mutations that would have to occur to transform that single-cell microscopic blob into a T. rex dinosaur.

However, those who reject the evolutionist's explanation in favor of the biblical account concerning the origin of life have allowed themselves to be painted into a corner that we should not have to reside in: the belief that the earth is only six thousand years old. I am constantly amazed at how many people believe that the Bible attempts to date the earth's age. Where did such an idea begin?

In 1654 an Anglican archbishop named James Ussher "proved" that the earth was created in 4004 BC. He arrived at this date by counting all the generations listed in the Bible, and then placed his dates in the margin of the King James Version of the Bible, leading many to believe that these dates were part of the original text.

However, Ussher's conclusions were based on several erroneous presuppositions. He claimed that (1) there are no undated verses in the Bible (yet the opening verse of the Bible has no date affixed to it), (2) there are no missing genealogies in the Bible (yet Matthew 1 omits many generations between Jesus, David, and Abraham), and (3) there are no historical gaps in the Bible (yet there is an obvious four-hundred-year gap between the Old and New Testaments). Ussher's flawed assumptions led to the highly doubtful theory that the earth is only six thousand years old.

How old *is* the earth? I don't have any idea. However, rejecting evolution does not require embracing the young Earth theory (the belief that the earth is only thousands of years old) because evolution seeks to answer the question "*How* did life begin?" rather than "*When* did life being?" For example, *Webster's New Collegiate Dictionary* defines *evolution* as "a theory that the various types of animals and plants have their origin in other preexisting types and that distinguishable differences are due to modifications in successive generations."

In other words, all life can be traced back to a one-celled living being (protozoan) from which every other life form has developed. Thus, zebras, birds, reptiles, chimpanzees, and human beings all originated from these unicellular creatures and are the result of slight variations (mutations) that occurred over billions of years.

The second major tenet of evolution is that *it requires major changes between species, not just minor variations within species.* As author Phillip Johnson points out, evolutionists love to use the old "bait and switch" routine to demonstrate the reality of evolution. For example, during the Kansas controversy described at the beginning of this chapter, reporter Jonathan Weiner wrote in the *Philadelphia Inquirer,* "Every time a farmer sprays pyrethroids and cotton moths go right on eating his cotton, that farmer is confronting evolution in action."[5] The reporter assumes that because moths develop resistance to pesticides over time, such a change proves the reality of evolution. The implication is, "Why do those hayseed Kansas creationists keep holding on to the Creation myth when evolution is right under their collective noses?"

The answer is, "Because there is a difference between microevolution (minor variations within species), which is observable and verifiable, and macroevolution (major variations between species), which is neither observable nor verifiable."

The evolutionist is skilled at baiting people to accept evolution by pointing to these minor changes that occur over time within species. For example, he will look at the differences in human beings and conclude, "The fact that human beings in America are larger today than they were a hundred years ago because of better nutrition proves the evolutionary hypothesis."

As writer Nancy Pearcey states in her article "We're Not in Kansas Anymore,"

Take an example that impressed Darwin: the variation in beak size among finches on the Galapagos Islands.... During a drought, the larger birds survived better and thus the average beak size increased slightly. Evolution in action? Not exactly. When the rains came back, beak sizes returned to normal. All that researchers discovered was a cyclical variation that allows finches to survive under changing conditions.[6]

Using these minor variations within species, the evolutionist theorizes that if such variations were compounded over millions of years, they would produce major variations such as reptiles evolving into birds and apes evolving into human beings.

But there is a huge difference between microevolution and macroevolution. For example, I came across a clipping in my files from a 1963 edition of a newspaper featuring an ad for a new Buick LeSabre automobile that was selling for $2,500. Have there been any changes between that model of car and a current model of the Buick LeSabre? Obviously, the passing of more than forty years has led to vast improvements in the efficiency and comfort of that model of automobile. The car has "evolved" over time.

However, such "evolution" in the car did not happen by accident. No matter how long you left a 1963 LeSabre in your garage, it would never develop a more efficient engine or a better shock system without the aid of an intelligent engineer. And even with the intervention of an engineer, the end result is still an automobile. That is microevolution.

However, if you left that 1963 Buick LeSabre in the garage for ten million years, is there any chance that it would ever evolve into a fully functioning 747 jetliner? Even with the intervention of an intelligent engineer, such a transformation would be impossible because there is a vast difference between a car and an airplane. That kind of macroevolution is just as improbable as the evolution of a reptile mutating into a bird or an ape morphing into a human being.

As we will explore further in the next section, there is not one scintilla of evidence anywhere that one species has ever evolved into another. Charles Darwin himself admitted in his memoir *My Life and Letters,* "Not one change of species into another is on record...we cannot prove that a single species has been changed."

Has the passing of more than one hundred years since Darwin

resulted in any "smoking gun" that proves macroevolution (changes between species)? Jerry Adler in *Newsweek* magazine notes, "The more scientists have searched for the transitional forms that lie between species, the more they have been frustrated."[7] In the next section we will discover that indeed there has been a great deal of paleontological evidence concerning macroevolution since the days of Charles Darwin, evidence that refutes rather than reinforces his theory.

Why would scientists cling with such tenacity to a theory like evolution that has so little corroborating evidence?

The third and final tenet of evolution is that *it is a religious philosophy that claims that Creation is the result of random chance rather than a Divine Designer.* Some misguided souls have tried to reconcile the *alleged* discrepancies between science and the Bible by proposing "theistic evolution." They theorize that God used the process of evolution to develop more complex life forms from simpler forms. So, to quote Rodney King, "Why can't we all just get along?" However, what theistic evolutionists fail to grasp is that evolution makes *no* allowance for a Creator-God.

While the evolutionist claims that her theory says nothing about the existence of God, it actually has a great deal to say about the role of God in the development of life. Evolution postulates that chance, not God, is responsible for the beginning of life. Furthermore, changes in life forms are the result of random mutations, not divine design. If you think I'm overstating the evolutionist's claim, consider this official 1995 position statement from the American National Association of Biology Teachers:

> The diversity of life on earth is the outcome of evolution: an unsupervised, impersonal, unpredictable and natural process of temporal descent with genetic modification that is affected by natural selection, chance, historical contingencies and changing environments.[8]

"Unsupervised...impersonal...unpredictable...and natural." These are the words that describe the origin of life according to the evolutionist. The philosophical pillar that undergirds evolution is *naturalism,* the philosophical belief that the universe is a closed system that cannot be influenced by anything or Anyone from the outside (such as God). The naturalist believes that nature is all there is. For the naturalist, any answer concerning the origin of life must be based on what he can see and measure. Yet, as we will see, evolution falls woefully short of these self-imposed restrictions.

Let me illustrate how ludicrous such a self-imposed limitation is. Suppose that in the 1700s someone theorized that some illnesses were caused by unicellular organisms that were incapable of being observed by the naked eye. The naturalist would have labeled such a claim outrageous since such organisms were unknown and unobservable. Yet in the 1800s French chemist Louis Pasteur discovered that organisms called bacteria are responsible for infection, and his work was responsible for the prevention of many contagious diseases. Thankfully, Pasteur did not allow naturalism to prevent him from discovering the truth.

Similarly, the fact that God cannot be seen by our eyes or measured by our instruments does not necessarily negate His existence—even by scientific criteria. Bacteria, molecules, and atoms all existed before human beings were able to view them. As Phillip Johnson notes, the problem with scientific naturalism is that it transforms "the limitations of science into limitations on reality."[9] The naturalist says that anything he cannot see or measure must not be real. (I wonder how the naturalist could persuade his mate that he loves her, since love can neither be seen nor measured.) Therefore, any theory of the origin of life must exclude the possibility of a Divine Creator since such a Creator cannot (yet) be seen.

This is crucial to understand. The naturalist seeks to exclude the possibility of a Divine Creator from the classroom (as in the Kansas case) by labeling her belief in naturalism as "science" and belief in a Divine Creator as "religious faith." According to the naturalist, science is objective and verifiable while religious faith is subjective and unverifiable. Therefore, the science of naturalism should be taught to everyone in the public schools, while religious faith in a Divine Creator should be relegated to the church or synagogue for the unenlightened who choose to embrace such a myth.

But is naturalism really good science? If you are sincerely trying to answer the question of the origin of life, can you truly be objective if you start with the premise that there is no God? Harvard biologist Richard Lewontin, in a 1997 article in *The New York Review of Books,* concedes that he is an evolutionist by default. Because of his commitment to materialism (another word for naturalism), he is forced to manufacture a theory for the origin of life that does not allow for the intervention of God:

> We are forced by our a priori adherence to material causes to
> create an apparatus of investigation and a set of concepts that
> produce material explanations.... Materialism is absolute, for we
> cannot allow a divine foot in the door.[10]

How's that for an objective quest for the truth? The point is obvious. The evolutionist would have you believe that those who believe in creationism are uneducated rubes incapable of scientific objectivity because they assume God's involvement in Creation. But the evolutionist is just as biased as the creationist because he comes to the table with the assumption that there is no God.

In fact, he is so vehement in his unobjective objection to God that he refuses to allow creationism to be offered as an alternative explanation and opposes any discussion of evolution's serious deficiencies. Why? Because acknowledging what science *really* reveals about the origin of life would point to an alternative explanation that is totally unacceptable to the naturalist.

Let's examine just a few of the *numerous* flaws in the theory of macroevolution that argue strongly for another explanation of the origin of life.

FOUR FATAL FLAWS OF EVOLUTION

1. The Problem of the Protein Molecule

Darwin theorized that all life forms are the result of slow changes (mutations) that have occurred over billions of years, beginning with one single-celled organism. A natural question would be, How did this single-celled creature come into existence? Or, as cosmologist Allan Sandage asks, "How is it that inanimate matter can organize itself to contemplate itself?"[11] The evolutionist will gloss over the question as quickly as possible because she has no answer for this greatest mystery of all. She will postulate that when chemicals that covered the earth—such as ammonia, methane, and hydrogen—were energized by lightening, amino acids (the building blocks of life) were produced. Those amino acids randomly assembled to produce protein molecules that eventually resulted in the first one-celled creature.

But even if we accept the idea that amino acids emerged from this prebiotic broth (a theory that is highly questionable), what are the chances of the correct amino acids randomly assembling together to produce a single protein molecule? Biochemist Michael Behe, author of

Darwin's Black Box, Dr. James Coppedge, an expert on statistical probability, and others estimate that "the probability of a single protein molecule being arranged by chance is 1 in 10^{161}."[12] That would be a one followed by one hundred sixty-one zeros. Such a number defies imagination, but Behe illustrates the remote probability such a number represents:

> Imagine that someone hid a grain of sand, marked with a tiny "x," somewhere in the Sahara Desert. After wandering blindfolded for several years in the desert you reach down, pick up a grain of sand, take off your blindfold, and find it has a tiny "x". Suspicious, you give the grain of sand to someone to hide again, again you wander blindfolded into the desert, bend down, and the grain you pick up again has an "x". A third time you repeat this action and a third time you find the marked grain. The odds of finding that marked grain of sand in the Sahara Desert three times in a row are about the same as finding one new functional protein structure.[13]

Dr. Coppedge offers another way to illustrate how much time it would take for amino acids to randomly assemble into a protein molecule. Envision an amoeba (a tiny one-celled organism) that decides to move the entire universe (every galaxy, solar system, planet, human, animal, and object contained in that universe) over the width of the entire universe. Because the amoeba is so small, it can only move objects atom by atom. So the amoeba starts with you, removes one Angstrom (the width of the hydrogen atom) of your body, and moves that atom to the other end of the universe. Since the universe is thirty billion light-years in diameter (a light-year is the distance light travels in a year at 186,282 miles per second), the amoeba must travel that distance carrying your one atom, deposit it on the other end of the universe, and then travel back the same distance and move the second atom.[14]

Think about how long it would take for that amoeba to transfer just one person, atom by atom, from one end of the universe to the other! But it must carry *every* human being, animal, plant, and object not only from this planet but from every planet in creation from one end of the universe to the other. According to Dr. Coppedge, the time it would take to accomplish such a feat would not even come close to the amount of time it would take to create just one protein molecule.[15] But even if that molecule were assembled by chance, you would then need a second molecule, and a third one. Obviously, the chance of such molecules forming randomly is zero. Yet the evolutionist prefers to place her faith in those kinds of odds rather than risk believing in a Divine Creator.

2. The Problem of the Black Box

To create life, however, you need more than one or two protein molecules "hooking up." A living cell would require bringing together hundreds of protein molecules to perform the necessary functions for supporting life. What are the chances of all those molecules randomly assembling together to form a single functioning cell? To answer that question, we first need to understand the complexity of the cell.

In his landmark book *The Origin of Species,* Darwin confessed one condition that would destroy his theory for the origin of life: "If it could be demonstrated that any complex organ existed which could not possibly have been formed by numerous, successive, slight modifications, my theory would absolutely break down."

When Darwin wrote these words, he and the other biologists of his day did not comprehend the complexity of the cell. They imagined the cell was a rather simple organism that could emerge from the primordial biotic soup by chance. The cell represented a "black box" to the nineteenth- and early-twentieth-century biologists, meaning that they had as little understanding about the complexities and workings of the cell as I have about what is going on inside the computer on which I am typing these words.

But after more than 150 years, and with the aid of powerful instruments, biologists have been able to peer into the cell's black box and view its enormous complexity. What they have discovered is that the molecular machinery and complicated systems the cell requires to function are far too complex to have evolved over a long period of time. Instead, according to Michael Behe in his seminal work *Darwin's Black Box*, the cell requires numerous systems to support life: "a functioning membrane, a system to build the DNA units, a system to control the copying of DNA, a system for energy processing," just to name a few.[16]

Now here's the key: All of these systems have to be present at the same time instead of being built gradually over a long period of time. To illustrate that requirement, Behe used the example of a mousetrap. A mousetrap requires five parts to catch mice—and all five must be fully functional from the beginning. Behe explained,

> You need all the parts to catch a mouse. You can't catch a few
> mice with a platform, then add the spring and catch a few more,
> and then add the hammer and improve its function. All the
> parts must be there to have any function at all. The mousetrap is
> irreducibly complex.[17]

In the same way, the cell requires that the aforementioned systems be in place all at once in order to function. Now remember what Darwin said about the Achilles heel of his theory: "If it could be demonstrated that any complex organ existed which could not possibly have been formed by numerous, successive, slight modifications, my theory would absolutely break down."

Why did Darwin offer such a concession? He understood that the chances of a complex organism's requiring numerous systems coming together at one time were about as great as putting all the pieces of a mousetrap in a washing machine and waiting for it to assemble itself from the agitation. No matter how long you waited, it would never happen.

But Darwin hung himself with his own words. Little did he know that science would one day discover such a "complex organ" (the cell) that could not have evolved slowly, but instead required complex and fully functioning systems from the beginning.

In the previous section we saw that the probability of amino acids' assembling themselves to form a protein molecule is 1 in 10^{161}. Now let's go one step further. What is the probability that a fully functioning cell would assemble itself together by chance? Sir Frederick Hoyle, an astronomer and mathematician from Cambridge University, writes, "The likelihood of the formation of life from inanimate matter is one to a number with 40,000 noughts [zeros] after it.... It is big enough to bury Darwin and the whole theory of evolution.... If the beginnings of life were not random, they must therefore have been the product of purposeful intelligence."[18]

Now you would think that in the more than 150 years since Darwin's writings, someone would have proposed a theory to explain the evolution of these complex systems. But after years of research, Behe has made an astounding discovery:

As you search the professional literature of the last several decades, looking for articles that have been published even attempting to explain the possible Darwinian step-by-step origin

of any of these systems, you will encounter thundering silence.
Absolutely no one—not one scientist—has published any
detailed proposal or explanation of the possible evolution of any
such complex biochemical system. And when a science does not
publish, it ought to perish.[19]

The complexity of the black box is another nail in evolution's cof-
fin. But there are more...

3. The Problem of Design

A famous parable describes a man walking through a field and discovering a stone. He walks a little further and stumbles upon an ornate gold
watch. The man may reasonably conclude that the stone has been there
for a long time and is simply the result of a sliver of mineral being
chipped away from the earth by chance. But the beauty, design, sym-
metry, and purpose represented in the gold watch could not have happened by chance. The watch must be the work of an intelligent and
purposeful Creator.[20]

Similarly, creation is filled with mechanisms much more intricately
designed than a watch, mechanisms that argue strongly for an intelligent and purposeful Creator. Because of space limitations, we will look
at just two of those mechanisms.

First, consider the DNA molecule. As molecular biologists began to
understand the design of the cell, they realized that protein molecules
were too complicated to have arisen by chance. There had to be some
source of information within the cell that could oversee the construc-
tion of these intricate mechanisms. In 1953 James Watson and Francis
Crick discovered the presence of a DNA molecule within every cell.

DNA stands for deoxyribonucleic acid and can be thought of as a microprocessor within each cell that contains all the information needed to regulate everything within that cell. A single fertilized egg of a human being, which is no larger than a pinhead, contains enough DNA information to fill 500,000 printed pages.[21] This information includes everything about you, including your hair color, height, the shape of your nose, the color of your skin, and every other detail about your body.

Over time, that single fertilized cell will divide into 30 trillion cells that make up your body, including 12 billion brain cells that form over 120 trillion connections.[22] The complicated set of instructions that guide that process is more than three *billion* letters long—and is contained in a single DNA molecule.[23]

Such a complex information system argues strongly for an Intelligent Designer. Stephen Meyer, an associate professor of philosophy at Whitworth College, explains it this way:

> Because mind or intelligent design is a necessary cause of an informative system, one can detect the past action of an intelligent cause from the presence of an information-intensive effect [such as the DNA molecule], even if the cause itself cannot be directly observed. Since information requires an intelligent source, the flowers spelling "Welcome to Victoria" in the gardens of Victoria Harbor [in Canada] lead visitors to infer the activity of intelligent agents even if they did not see the flowers planted and arranged.[24]

When one understands the complexity of the DNA information system, it becomes clear that such a system requires a Programmer. As author Charles Thaxton argues, "An intelligible communication via radio signal from some distant galaxy would be widely hailed as evidence of an intelligent source. Why then doesn't the message sequence on the DNA molecule also constitute prima facie evidence for an intelligent source?"[25]

Sir Francis Crick, who discovered the DNA molecule, came to the same conclusion—well, sort of. Unwilling to admit the possibility of a Creator-God, Crick theorized that perhaps life spores were sent to Earth by an advanced civilization from another planet. Phillip Johnson, author of *Defeating Darwinism,* exposes the desperation of such an "explanation" when he says, "When a scientist of Crick's caliber feels he has to invoke undetectable spacemen, it is time to consider whether the field of prebiological evolution has come to a dead end."[26]

Let's move beyond the intricacies of proteins, cells, and DNA molecules to something we can all see, so to speak: the human eye. The eye is composed of a ball containing a lens on one side and, on the other, a light sensitive retina that consists of rods and cones. The lens is protected by a covering called the cornea and rests on an iris that is designed to protect the cornea from excessive light.

Every four hours, a watery substance within the eye is replaced, while tear glands continually flush the outside of the eye clean. Every eye also contains a "windshield wiper" called the eyelid that spreads a special secretion over the cornea to keep it moist and to protect the eye from dust.[27]

If that is not complicated enough, the eye is not an island unto itself. As light hits the human eye, billions of bits of information travel from the eye through millions of nerve fibers that are linked to the brain.[28] There, at "information central" in the visual cortex of the brain, that data is processed and then dispatched to various parts of your body with instructions such as "Tell hands to close the book because this is too complicated."

Seriously, how does evolution account for the development of such a complex organ as the eye? Darwin's answer will absolutely dumbfound you:

> To suppose that the eye with all its inimitable contrivances for adjusting the focus to different distances, for admitting different amounts of light and for the correction of spherical and chromatic aberration, could have been formed by natural selection, seems, I freely confess, absurd in the highest degree.[29]

At least Darwin was honest! When you consider the intricate design of living systems, you come to the same conclusion as the psalmist, who exclaimed, "The fool has said in his heart, 'There is no God'" (Psalm 14:1).

Let's look at just one more flaw in the evolutionist's theory that will probably surprise you.

4. The Fossil Problem

If indeed all life forms as we know them are the result of slight modifications over billions of years, then there should be a multitude of evidence in the fossil record of simple organisms evolving into complex organisms. In fact, you probably assume that such a mountain of evidence exists, causing creationists a great deal of embarrassment. *Wrong!* Dr. Gary Parker, a biologist and a former evolutionist, notes the thundering silence from the fossil record:

> In most people's minds, fossils and Evolution go hand in hand.
> In reality, fossils are a great embarrassment to Evolutionary
> theory and offer strong support for the concept of Creation. If

Evolution were true, we should find literally millions of fossils that show how one kind of life slowly and gradually changed to another kind of life. But missing links are the trade secret, in a sense, of palaeontology.[30]

Remember, evolution is not only about slight modifications within a species over a long period of time. Instead, the evolutionist is claiming that those tiny changes added up to huge changes between species, such as reptiles evolving into birds or mammals evolving into human beings. But if such macrochanges actually occurred, why is there no fossil record of single-celled organisms changing step-by-step into more complex plants and animals?

The evolutionist answers by saying that the fossil record is incomplete and, in time, such evidence will appear. However, if all that were needed was more fossils, then you would suppose that there would be evolutionary evidence where fossils are most abundant—among marine invertebrates. Yet Dr. Niles Eldredge, an evolutionist and leading expert on invertebrate fossils, admits that the opposite is true:

> No wonder paleontologists shied away from evolution for so long. It seems never to happen. Assiduous collecting up cliff faces yields zigzags, minor oscillations, and the very occasional slight accumulation of change—over millions of years, at a rate too slow to really account for all the prodigious change that has occurred in evolutionary history.[31]

However, much to the evolutionist's dismay, the fossil record does support a "sudden" appearance of all major life forms. The cover of a *Time* article titled "When Life Exploded" stated that "new discoveries show that life as we know it began in an amazing biological frenzy that changed the planet almost overnight."[32] The article was referring to what paleontologists call the "Cambrian explosion."

A little background is helpful here. Many evolutionists believe that the earth is approximately 4.5 billion years old. For the first 700 million years of its existence, the earth was the victim of a continuous bombardment by meteorites. The evolutionist theorizes that within 100 million years of the cessation of the meteorite showers, the first life form appeared out of the primordial broth of chemicals that covered the earth. As we have seen, the evolutionist has no explanation for how this simple yet amazingly complex single-celled life form emerged—but that's another story.

For the next 3 billion years, the earth was populated with these single-celled creatures. But suddenly, during the Cambrian geological period (500–570 million years ago), all the known phyla (the next largest subcategory) of the animal kingdom appeared, with the exception of one. Furthermore, all of these different animals appear in the fossil record without any ancestors or intermediates.

Instead, this evidently occurred over a time period of "only" 5 to 10 million years.[33] To us that seems like eternity, but to the evolutionist it is only a blink of an eye. Why? Evolution is based on the premise of slight changes over a long period of time. If an organism were to change too rapidly, it would not fit its environment and would die. Even the late, ardent evolutionist Stephen Jay Gould of Harvard University was surprised by the rapidity of development evidenced in the Cambrian period, admitting, "Fast is now a lot faster than we thought, and that is extraordinarily interesting."[34] The same *Time* article quotes paleontologist Samuel Bowring as saying, "We now know how fast fast is. And what I like to ask my biologist friends is, 'How fast can evolution get before they start feeling uncomfortable?'"[35]

Equally significant is the fact that since this "explosion" nearly 500 million years ago, during which nearly all the major animal groups suddenly appeared, there has been little change in those animal groups. If macroevolution is a fact, wouldn't we have seen some evidence of it during the last 500 million years?

Think about this: If the fossil record demonstrates that all the major animal groups suddenly appeared with no ancestors and intermediates and, furthermore, that there have been no drastic changes since that time, what is the fossil record *really* saying to us?

You would think that the evolutionist would offer a plausible explanation for the sudden appearance of all these animal groups in a short amount of time. But he can't. As *Time* magazine points out,

> Of course, understanding what made the Cambrian explosion possible doesn't address the larger question of what made it happen so fast. Here scientists delicately slide across data—thin ice, suggesting scenarios that are based on intuition rather than solid evidence.[36]

Reread that last sentence carefully. It pictures the evolutionist as ignoring the clear evidence from the fossil record of a Creator and instead grabbing for any other explanation for the origin of life. The evolutionist's explanations are not based on any evidence, but on his "intuition," an intuition that is built on the premise that there is no God.

FINAL THOUGHTS

As we conclude this chapter, allow me to offer three suggestions for dealing with those who view the evolutionary theory as an undeniable fact of science.

First, distinguish between microevolution and macroevolution. Minor changes within species such as birds, horses, and humans are abundantly evident within nature. But evolution is not just about minor variations; it is about major changes within species (such as the development of a leg or a brain) and major changes between species (a monkey becoming a human being). While the evidence for microevolution is plentiful, the evidence for macroevolution is nonexistent. If, as evolutionists claim, these minor changes add up to major changes, then why have there been no new *major* animal groups since the Cambrian explosion 500 million years ago?

Second, don't be dazzled by new "discoveries." Because paleoanthropologists (those who study human fossils) are fervently searching for evidence to support the evolutionary hypothesis, they tend to interpret the fossil record selectively.

For example, in his book *Bones of Contention,* Marvin Lubenow recounts the amazing case of Skull 1470, a human skull found in rock that had been dated at 2.9 million years. Since, according to the evolutionists' timetable, such a highly developed skull could not have existed that long ago, the rock's age was changed to 1.9 million years old, which better coincided with the date of human evolution—a date that in turn was based on the "certainty" of the date of the evolution of pigs. Lubenow writes, "The pigs won.... The pigs took it all. But in reality, it wasn't the pigs that won. It was evolution that won. In the dating game, evolution always wins."[37] If the fossil record seems to substantiate the evolutionists' claim, it is accepted. If it doesn't, then the age of the fossil is simply changed to fit the "fact" of evolution. Such selectivity should make all of us dubious of claims based on fossil discoveries.

Evolutionists are so desperate to support their theory that they often have to make embarrassing retractions. For example, for many years evolutionists believed that Nebraska man was the oldest example of the human species, dating back to one million years ago. In the famous Scopes trial of 1925 that dealt with the teaching of evolution in Tennessee, the existence of Nebraska man was presented as irrefutable proof of evolution. What was the origin of this remarkable "discovery"? A man named Harold Cook discovered a tooth—not a set of teeth, but a single tooth—in Nebraska. From that single tooth, paleoanthropologists extrapolated and invented an entire man, and an entire race was named as a result of this discovery.

However, years after the Scopes trial, the entire skeleton of this creature was unearthed. But instead of a human being, it was a pig! An entire new race of human beings was built on the tooth of a pig! If space allowed, I could point to other such embarrassments to evolutionists such as Java man, the Heidelberg jaw, Piltdown man, and Neanderthal man. All of these represented landmark "discoveries" at the time that later had to be retracted.

The point is simple: Don't allow headlines proclaiming a new anthropological discovery to sway your thinking. The conclusions from such findings are as changeable as the shifting sand in which they are discovered. Evolutionist and fossil expert Stephen Jay Gould candidly admitted, "The fossil record with its abrupt transitions offers no support for gradual change."[38]

Finally, refuse to fall into the science-versus-the-Bible trap. The evolutionist wants to categorize his theory as objective and incontrovertible "science" and your belief in a Creator-God as subjective religious belief. Not so fast. As I pointed out earlier, the evolutionist's theory has no scientific explanation for some basic questions such as

- How did protein molecules assemble from amino acids?
- Since a living cell could not have evolved but requires all of its part to be operational at once, how do you explain its origin?

- Why is there no fossil evidence of unicellular creatures evolving into complex plants and animals?

Furthermore, it is erroneous to assume that believing in a Divine Designer is illogical simply because we cannot see that Designer. Since when has reality been limited to what we can "see"? For thousands of years man could not see atoms, molecules, and bacteria, and yet they existed. We should not allow our limitations to define reality.

Remember, the evolutionist stacks the deck in the argument by automatically labeling naturalism as "science." Since naturalism is limited to what is observable and measurable, then it is impossible for a naturalist to involve God in creation since He is neither. By such a sleight of hand, the evolutionist immediately eliminates the possibility of a Divine Creator. Don't allow her to get away with that! If *science* is defined as that which is observable and repeatable, then neither evolution nor Creation can be treated as scientific fact since they both purport to explain a process that no one has observed. While science can tell us a great deal about how certain things (like the eye) work, it cannot tell us how such a complicated organ came into being.

Any discussion of the origin of life begins with a presupposition about God and His role in creation. The evolutionist's assumption that there is no Divine Creator is just as much a religious philosophy as the assumption that there is. The real question is this: "To which assumption do the footprints of this complex universe lead us?"

Dr. H. S. Lipson, a physicist and self-avowed agonistic, concludes, "I think...the only acceptable explanation is creation.... I know that this is anathema to physicists, as indeed it is to me, but we must not reject a theory that we do not like if the experimental evidence supports it.... To my mind the theory [evolution] does not stand up at all."[39]

America Is a Christian Nation

I n June 2002 the U.S. Court of Appeals for the Ninth Circuit ruled that the Pledge of Allegiance to the United States flag cannot be recited in public schools because the phrase "under God" is a violation of the constitutional separation of church and state. In its ruling the court said, "To recite the pledge is not to describe the United States; instead, it is to swear allegiance to the values for which the flag stands: unity, indivisibility, liberty, justice and—since 1954—monotheism [the belief in one God]."[1]

In April 2002 a member of the Joes, Colorado, school board introduced a proposal requiring that area schools offer a balanced treatment of evolution and science. After being threatened with litigation from the Americans United for Separation of Church and State, the school board defeated the proposal by a 5-0 vote. Barry Lynn, executive director of Americans United for Separation of Church and State, claimed that schools may not "promote religious doctrine thinly disguised as science. It is unconstitutional to turn our public schools into Sunday schools."[2]

On July 4, 1998, the pastor of a Southern Baptist church preached a patriotic sermon on the Christian heritage of our nation and, without endorsing any candidate, urged Christians to select leaders who are committed to God and His Word. As a result, a liberal watchdog group threatened his church's tax-exempt status, claiming that such comments amounted to "church politicking" and were in violation of federal tax laws.

I am most familiar with the last case because I was the pastor involved. In the midst of the library-book controversy I described at the beginning of this book, I preached a message on the Fourth of July weekend titled "One Nation Under Siege." In that sermon I recounted the strong Christian heritage of our nation, our defection from that legacy as evidenced by countless court rulings that have removed any acknowledgment of God from the public arena, and what I believed were the direct effects of such a departure on our society. I closed the message with several practical applications, including praying for our nation, taking advantage of our privilege to vote, and electing leaders who are committed to biblical principles:

> The purpose of the church is not to clean up society. There is
> no more futile ministry in the world than to try to keep sinners
> from sinning—you just can't do it. Our job is to preach the
> gospel of Christ and to make disciples of Christ. But there comes
> a time when Christians must band together. There comes a time
> when we should vote out these infidels who would deny God
> and His Word.

It was that last phrase, "vote out these infidels," that sent groups like People for the American Way, the American Civil Liberties Union, the Baptist Joint Committee on Public Affairs, and Americans United for Separation of Church and State into apoplexy. In their response to my message, the ACLU never once refuted any of the historical documentation I cited regarding the Christian heritage of our nation, but instead said, "As a people, we have always rejected this type of religious intolerance and bigotry." Barry Lynn FedExed a letter to me (which he also simultaneously sent to numerous news outlets around the country) saying, "Your comments about how your congregation should vote in the next election raise serious legal questions.... You are placing the tax-exempt status of your congregation in jeopardy."[3]

The only problem with Lynn's threat was that I never once referred to any upcoming election (the next city council election was a year away), much less endorsed any candidate. Phil Beasley, a spokesman for the IRS, said in a *Times Record News* interview on July 11, 1998, "As long as they [our church] don't intervene in any political campaign, they are well within in their rights."

There are countless other examples of attempts to remove the acknowledgment of God from public life, ranging from banning nativity scenes on government property to prohibiting prayer at high-school football games. All of these efforts to secularize our society have one thing in common: They are based on the principle of the separation of church and state.

Listen long enough to the arguments of the American Civil Liberties Union or Americans United for Separation of Church and State, and you will become convinced that the bedrock principle for the founding of our country was government's neutrality (which is better translated "hostility") toward all things religious. Our forefathers, we are told, came to this country from diverse religious backgrounds. Some were Christians, others were deists, but most were secularists who believed that religion was fine as long as it was confined to the church and home. Supposedly our nation's founders were determined to build an unscalable wall that would keep any religious influence from seeping into public life.

Yet that version of American history belongs in the same category as the story of George Washington and the cherry tree. It is a myth. As we will discover, the majority of our nation's founders were not religionists, but Christians. They did not embrace many faiths, but they were devout followers of the Christian faith.

Furthermore, the early leaders of our nation believed that the foundation of our nation's laws should be the eternal principles found in the Bible. Though it is politically incorrect to voice such a belief, it is nevertheless true: America was founded as a Christian nation, and her continued success will be determined by her fidelity to her spiritual heritage.

LET THE RECORD SPEAK

I realize that such a claim runs contrary to the revisionist version of history that is regularly regurgitated in classrooms and on talk shows across the nation, so let's allow the historical record to speak for itself.

First, let's consider the spiritual beliefs of the men who were responsible for framing our U.S. Constitution. Were they neutral toward religion in general and the Christian faith in particular? Hardly! Fifty-three of the fifty-six men who attended the Constitutional Convention and formulated our nation's guiding document "indicated some adherence to orthodox Christianity and personal support of biblical teaching." In fact, some of these same men were responsible for establishing the American Bible Society, the American Tract Society, and the Philadelphia Bible Society.[4]

To attend the Constitutional Convention, each delegate had to meet qualifications established by his respective state—qualifications that were only a few years old at the time of the Constitutional Convention. Read carefully the requirements contained in the Delaware Constitution of 1776:

Art. 22. Every person who shall be chosen a member of either
house, or appointed to any office or place of trust...shall...make
and subscribe to the following declaration, to wit: "I...do profess
faith in God the Father, and in Jesus Christ His only Son, and
in the Holy Ghost, one God, blessed for evermore; and I do
acknowledge the holy scriptures to the Old and New Testament
to be given by divine inspiration."[5]

Other states had similar qualifications for those who were selected
to attend the Constitutional Convention. Furthermore, as David Barton
points out, these state constitutions that required officeholders to be
Christians were written by the very men who were chosen to attend the
Constitutional Convention.[6] The point is obvious: Those individuals
who were responsible for penning our nation's founding document were
hardly neutral toward Christianity!

A few years ago two professors from the University of Houston, Don-
ald Lutz and Charles Hyneman, wanted to discover whom our Founding
Fathers quoted most often. Obviously, the answer to such a question was
important in determining the influences that shaped their thinking and
would be like a Rosetta stone that might aid in interpreting their writings.

After ten years of studying more than 15,000 documents, they
found that the three men our Founding Fathers quoted most often were
British philosopher John Locke, French philosopher Baron Montesquieu,
and English judge Sir William Blackstone. However, our Founding
Fathers cited the Bible four times more than they quoted Montesquieu
or Blackstone and twelve times more than they quoted John Locke.
More than a third of all the Founding Fathers' quotes came directly
from the Bible, and another 60 percent came from those authors who
had based their writings on the Bible.[7]

For example, did you know that the separation of governmental powers prescribed in the Constitution is based on Isaiah 33:22: "For the LORD is our judge, the LORD is our lawgiver, the LORD is our king"? From this verse our forefathers established the judicial, legislative, and executive branches of government. Such a separation of powers, our Founding Fathers reasoned, was mandated by man's innate corruption described in Jeremiah 17:9: "The heart is deceitful above all things, and desperately wicked; who can know it?" (NKJV). Furthermore, the idea of granting tax-exempt status to churches and religious organizations is based on Ezra 7:24, which commanded special financial consideration for the building of the temple.[8]

By looking at the ideas and influences that shaped our Founding Fathers' thinking, we can clearly see that the Bible played a crucial role in the formation of our government. Ken Woodward, writing for *Newsweek* magazine in an article titled "How the Bible Made America," said, "Now historians are discovering that the Bible, perhaps even more than the Constitution, is our founding document."[9]

Read carefully the testimony of those men who through their sacrifice and tears gave birth to our nation. George Washington, our first president, wrote in his prayer journal:

> Let my heart, gracious God, be so affected with Your glory and majesty that I may...discharge those weighty duties which Thou requirest of me.... I have called on Thee for pardon and forgiveness of sins...for the sacrifice of Jesus Christ offered upon the cross for me.... thou gav'st thy Son to die for me; and hast given me assurance of salvation.[10]

At his inaugural address, the first in our nation's history, Washington was compelled to acknowledge God's role in the founding of our country:

It would be peculiarly improper to omit in this first official Act, my fervent supplications to that Almighty Being.... No People can be bound to acknowledge and adore the invisible hand which conducts the Affairs of men more than the People of the United States. Every step, by which they have advanced to the character of an independent nation, seems to have been distinguished by some...providential agency.... We ought to be no less persuaded that the propitious smiles of Heaven, can never be expected on a nation that disregards the eternal rules of order and right, which Heaven itself has ordained.[11]

Or consider the words of the second president of the United States, John Adams:

The general principles, on which the Fathers achieved independence, were...the general Principles of Christianity.... I will avow, that I then believed, and now believe, that those general Principles of Christianity, are as eternal and immutable, as the Existence and Attributes of God; and that those Principles of Liberty, are as unalterable as human Nature.[12]

Patrick Henry, a leader of the American Revolution and, later, one of the primary influencers responsible for adding the Bill of Rights to the Constitution, is best known for his famous declaration, "Give me liberty or give me death." But there is another utterance of Henry's that you don't hear historians quoting because it is a politically incorrect though absolutely accurate assessment of the founding of our nation: "It cannot be emphasized too strongly or too often that this great nation was founded, not by religionists, but by Christians, not on religions, but on the gospel of Jesus Christ."[13]

I want you to go back and reread that statement. Isn't that diametrically opposed to what our children are learning in school today? The historical revisionists insist that our country's forefathers came from a diversity of religious beliefs. Wrong! Although some were Methodists, others Presbyterians, and others Congregationalists, they were primarily Christians. There were no Muslims on the Mayflower! And because their faith was an integral part of their lives, it was only natural that our ancestors built their dream of a new nation on the bedrock of Christianity. John Quincy Adams, sixth president of the United States and son of President John Adams, who was a leader in the American Revolution and a signer of the Declaration of Independence, offered this assessment of the linkage between Christianity and the founding of our country: "The highest glory of the American Revolution was this; it connected, in one indissoluble bond, the principles of civil government and the principles of Christianity."[14]

Christianity and civil government "connected in one indissoluble bond"? Wait a minute! Someone call the ACLU immediately! What about the separation of church and state? Don't the words of John Adams, Patrick Henry, and George Washington contradict what many believe is the cornerstone belief of our nation: government's neutrality toward religion?

THE MYTH OF SEPARATION

I am amazed by the number of people who are convinced that the phrase "wall of separation of church and state" is part of the United States Constitution. It's been reported that a significant majority of Americans believe that this oft-quoted phrase is contained in the First Amendment to the Constitution.[15] They are shocked when they discover that not only is it *not* found in the First Amendment, it is not found *anywhere* in the Constitution. Then where did this phrase originate and what does it mean?

In 1801 a group of Baptists in Connecticut were alarmed over a rumor that was spreading throughout the Northeast that the Congregational denomination was about to be established as the national denomination of the United States. In other words, Baptists, Presbyterians, Methodists, and other denominations would be deemed inferior or would be outlawed altogether. Their concern went beyond the usual paranoia we Baptists feel when we think some other group might get an upper hand. They had heard horror stories from their parents and grandparents about state-established religion in England. Those who had refused to follow the dictates of the Church of England were subjected to imprisonment and torture. So they fled England not to be free *from* religion, but to have freedom *of* religious expression.

Naturally, when this first generation of Americans heard that quite possibly there was about to be a Church of the United States, they were understandably alarmed. As a result they contacted then-president Thomas Jefferson about the rumor. Jefferson allayed their fears in a letter addressed to the Danbury Baptists on January 1, 1802:

> I contemplate with sovereign reverence that act of the whole American people which declared that their legislature should "make no law respecting an establishment of religion, or prohibiting the free exercise thereof," thus building a wall of separation between Church and State.[16]

If Jefferson's phrase "separation between Church and State" did not come from the Constitution, where did it originate? Remember, Jefferson was addressing a group of Baptists, and like any good politician, he invoked the words of someone his audience could identify with. In this case, Jefferson recited the words of Roger Williams, a prominent Baptist preacher and the founder of Rhode Island, who had said:

> When they have opened a gap in the hedge or wall of Separation between the Garden of the Church and the Wildernes of the world, God hath ever broke down the wall it selfe...and that therfore if he will ever please to restore his Garden and Paradice again, it must of necessitie be walled in peculiarly unto himselfe from the world.[17]

In Williams's mind, the danger to be avoided at all costs was not the church influencing the world, but the world influencing and corrupting the church. Thus, the "wall" Williams had in mind was a wall built to protect the church from the world, not to protect the world from the church.

Similarly, Thomas Jefferson used Williams's words to reassure those Connecticut Baptists that the First Amendment was established not to protect government from the church, but to protect the church from government. New scholarship surrounding Jefferson's letter to the Danbury Baptists reveals that Jefferson worked with his political advisors to carefully craft this letter in order to gain the support of these New England Baptists where the rival Federalist political party was deeply entrenched.[18]

Understanding Jefferson's purpose in using the phrase "separation between Church and State" is key to understanding its meaning. When Barry Lynn invoked that phrase in his letter to me, he did so to threaten a group of Baptists with loss of their tax-exempt status. His purpose was to *restrict* religious expression. But clearly, Jefferson used the phrase "separation between Church and State" to *reassure* this group of believers that government would never restrain their religious freedom by mandating one state-sponsored denomination.

Jefferson was simply echoing the promise in the First Amendment to the Constitution, ratified thirteen years later, that promised "Congress shall make no law respecting the establishment of religion or prohibiting the free exercise thereof." Never in their wildest imaginations did Jefferson or the framers of the Constitution envision that the First Amendment would be used as a rationale for separating our nation from its Christian foundation.

How can I say that with such assurance? First, consider Thomas Jefferson's own actions and words. One year after writing the above-quoted letter containing the phrase "separation between Church and State," President Jefferson recommended that the United States Congress sign a treaty with the Kaskaskia Indians that included government financial support of missionaries to the Indians and declared that certain parcels of land be reserved for "Christian Indians." On three separate occasions during his administration, Jefferson reaffirmed this arrangement with the Indians. (Had they been around at the time, I am confident that the ACLU and the Americans United for Separation of Church and State would have filed a suit against Thomas Jefferson.) Why did Jefferson promote such an arrangement? He understood the importance of integrating government and Christianity. He said that religion is "deemed in other countries incompatible with good government and yet proved by our experience to be its best support."[19]

Second, consider what early court rulings said about the relationship between government and Christianity. In countless cases during the first 140 years of our nation, the judiciary reaffirmed our country's Christian foundation and encouraged government's support of the Christian faith.

For example, in the case of *Runkel v. Winemiller* (1799), the Supreme Court of Maryland said in its decision, "By our form of government, the

Christian religion is the established religion; and all sects and denominations of Christians are placed upon the same equal footing, and are equally entitled to protection in their religious liberty."[20] The court said that our nation has an established religion, and it is Christianity! Were the justices ignorant of the First Amendment that had been ratified just nine years earlier promising that "Congress shall make no law regarding the establishment of a religion"? Of course not! In fact, these justices were in a much better position to understand what the framers of the Constitution had in mind than those of us who live hundreds of years after the fact. If they had any question about the meaning of the First Amendment's "establishment clause," the Maryland justices were free to consult personally with those who drafted the amendment, since they were contemporaries.

The justices of the Maryland Supreme Court realized that the First Amendment was about protecting religious liberty, not restricting religious expression. Like Thomas Jefferson, they interpreted the prohibition against Congress's establishing a "religion" as referring to government's preference of one Christian denomination over another Christian denomination. But that restriction in no way denied the Christian heritage of our nation.

Nearly one hundred years later, the United States Supreme Court reaffirmed our nation's Christian foundation in *Church of the Holy Trinity v. United States* (1892). This case dealt with a church's being sued by the government for employing a pastor from England, which supposedly violated a federal immigration law. The United States Supreme Court rejected such an application of the law to the church. In its ruling the Supreme Court declared, "No purpose of action against religion can be imputed to any legislation, state or national, because this is a religious people.... This is a Christian nation."[21]

In its sixteen-page decision, the Court supported that contention by quoting from a variety of previous court decisions such as *The People v. Ruggles* (1811) in which the Chief Justice of the New York Supreme Court affirmed, "We are a Christian people, and the morality of the country is deeply engrafted upon Christianity, and not upon the doctrines of worship of those imposters [other religions]."[22]

The Supreme Court of the United States not only declared that America is a Christian nation but, by quoting the New York decision, deemed other religions as "imposter" religions! Have you ever heard this case cited in any civics course you have taken? Author David Moore claims that there is not a law textbook in use today that discusses *Holy Trinity v. United States*. Why not? It is not because this case is unimportant. In 1991 Justice John Paul Stevens referred to this case as having "controlling precedent," meaning that it is still relevant today.[23] The reason this case has been buried is the same reason our children do not hear about the Christian faith of our forefathers and their desire to build this nation upon the principles of Christianity: In today's culture of diversity, it is politically incorrect to say that America was founded on the principles of Christianity, not the principles of Islam, Buddhism, or any other "imposter" religion.

Despite the attempt by some to ignore the *Holy Trinity* case, it is impossible to disregard the strong manner in which the Supreme Court, as well as other courts, strongly affirmed our nation's Christian heritage. The case of *Vidal v. Girard's Executors* (1844) is of particular interest. This complicated case dealt with a man (Stephen Girard) who left his estate to the City of Philadelphia for the establishment of a college. In his will Girard stipulated that the professors seek to instill principles of morality in the students without any reference to the Bible or Christianity. (Sound familiar?) Read carefully the unanimous opinion of the Supreme Court of the United States in rejecting the notion of separating morality from Christianity:

Christianity...is not to be maliciously and openly reviled and
blasphemed against, to the annoyance of believers or the injury
of the public.... It is unnecessary for us, however, to consider
the establishment of a school or college, for the propagation
of...Deism, or any other form of infidelity. Such a case is not
to be presumed to exist in a Christian country.[24]

I need to stop here and fast-forward 160 years to the debate that is
raging today concerning the teaching of sexual abstinence to teenagers
in the public schools. The ACLU and other groups are violently
opposed to such instruction because they claim that sexual abstinence
has a religious foundation and therefore violates the sacred separation of
church and state. They argue that if such a Christian-based idea (which,
by the way, is not exclusively Christian) is allowed in the schools, what
is to prevent Buddhists or even Satan worshipers from insisting that
their view of sexuality be presented in the classroom?

Unfortunately some well-meaning Christians wilt under that argument and conclude, "If Buddhism were the prevalent religion in our
country, I would not want my child to have to endure in the classroom a
Buddhist perspective on sexuality. Perhaps 'religion' should stay out of the
classroom altogether." And so they become accomplices in this determined effort to sanitize the classroom from anything that smacks of
Christianity.

But understand what the Supreme Court said in 1844—just forty
years after Jefferson's famous "separation-between-Church-and-State"
letter. In *Vidal v. Girard's Executors* the justices said the argument of
parity was fallacious. One does *not* have to treat all religions equally in
the classroom. Why not? Because other religions (like deism) are "infi-
delities." America is "a Christian country," the Court affirmed!

It is interesting to note that the Chief Justice of the Supreme Court who delivered this opinion for the entire court was Justice Joseph Story, who had been appointed to the Court by President James Madison, the man considered by many to have been the chief architect of the United States Constitution. Obviously, Madison would only have appointed Story to the bench if he felt Story had a clear understanding of the Constitution. For Justice Story, declaring America a Christian nation and elevating Christianity above every other religion in no way contradicted the liberties promised in the First Amendment. Again, who was in a better position to understand the intent of our Founding Fathers: those who were their contemporaries or those who lived 160 years after the fact?

Furthermore, the Supreme Court reasoned that since this is a Christian nation, we should not hesitate to teach the Bible to our students to encourage moral behavior:

> Why may not the Bible, and especially the New Testament,
> without note or comment, be read and taught as a divine
> revelation in the [school]—its general precepts expounded,
> its evidences explained and its glorious principles of morality
> inculcated?... Where can the purest principles of morality be
> learned so clearly or so perfectly as from the New Testament?[25]

According to the Supreme Court, attempting to separate the teaching of Christianity from the teaching of morality was not only impossible, it was unnecessary since this is a Christian nation.

During the first 160 years of our nation's history, public-school students were encouraged to learn the moral precepts found in the Bible. For example, in 1782 the United States Congress said, "The Congress of the United States approves and recommends to the people the Holy Bible for use in the schools." For nearly two hundred years, *The New England Primer* was used in schools across the land. That primer contained an acrostic every child had to memorize in order to graduate from the third grade. Every letter in the acrostic was related to a verse from the Bible:

A—"A wise son maketh a glad father, but a foolish son is the heaviness of his mother."

B—"Better is a little with the fear of the Lord, than great treasure & trouble therewith."

C—"Come unto Christ all ye that labor and are heavy laden and he will give you rest."

D—" 'Do not do the abominable thing which I hate,' saith the Lord."

E—"Except a man be born again, he cannot see the kingdom of God."[26]

Can you imagine such a textbook being adopted today by a school board? As we saw in chapter 6, any textbook that dares suggest the existence of a Creator-God is angrily denounced and excluded from consideration.

So what happened to cause such a seismic shift in sentiment toward Christianity in public life? Some will point to Supreme Court cases in the early 1960s that removed Bible reading and then prayer from the classroom. But the genesis of this change in attitude occurred fifteen years earlier.

CONSTRUCTING THE WALL

The first time the U.S. Supreme Court declared that the First Amendment had "erected a wall of separation between church and state" and that the duty of the Court was to ensure that the "wall…be kept high and impregnable" was in the case of *Everson v. Board of Education* in 1947—150 years after the ratification of the First Amendment. In this landmark case the Supreme Court forbade the State of New Jersey to expend tax dollars for religious education. The guiding force behind this decision was Justice Hugo Black who cited Jefferson's "wall of separation" in his majority opinion. American University professor Daniel Dreisbach and University of Chicago law professor Philip Hamburger claim that the iron curtain Justice Black erected between Christianity and government had little to do with Thomas Jefferson and the Constitution. "What we have today is not really Jefferson's wall, but Supreme Court Justice Hugo Black's wall," according to Professor Dreisbach. "You can't understand the period when Justice Black was on the court without understanding the fear American elites had of Catholic influence and power."[27] (Remember that in those days nearly all parochial schools were Catholic.)

Professor Hamburger notes that Justice Black's anti-Catholic bias was no doubt due to Black's former membership in the Ku Klux Klan, which was noted for its bigotry against Catholicism. Thus, the professor concludes, his desire to build a "high and impregnable" wall between the church and state was really a desire to build a wall between the Catholic church and the rest of society.[28]

Two current members of the Supreme Court agree. Supreme Court Justices Clarence Thomas and Antonin Scalia have recently argued that the rabid desire to wall off "sectarian" groups from government support was founded upon anti-Catholic bigotry. "It was an open secret that 'sectarian' was a code for 'Catholic.' This doctrine, born of bigotry, should be buried now," Justice Thomas wrote in a recent court opinion.[29]

By the way, if the separation of church and state was such a foundational concept in the founding of our nation, why didn't the phrase appear in the *World Book Encyclopedia* until 1967? Because the wall—as it is applied today—was not erected by our nation's forefathers, but by those who are seeking to secularize our nation and separate it from its Christian heritage.

THE WALL GROWS HIGHER

Since the *Everson* case in 1947, the courts have succeeded in accomplishing Black's goal of keeping the wall of separation high and impregnable. In the case of *Engel v. Vitale* in 1962, the Court ruled that students in New York could no longer recite this simple twenty-two-word voluntary prayer: "Almighty God, we acknowledge our dependence upon Thee, and we beg Thy blessings upon us, our parents, our teachers, and our Country."[30]

Although this innocuous prayer (described by one person as a to-whomever-it-may-concern prayer) promoted no particular denomination, the Supreme Court declared it unconstitutional, claiming that it breached "the constitutional wall of separation between church and state."[31] But the Court did not stop there. The justices went on to opine about the relationship between government and Christianity: "A union of government and religion tends to destroy government and to degrade religion."[32]

Yet 160 years earlier John Quincy Adams had declared that the highest glory of the American Revolution was that it connected in "one indissoluble bond the principles of civil government and Christianity." The judiciary's dramatic shift away from the Founding Fathers' intentions is obvious to anyone.

Ironically, the United States Congress begins every session with prayer. Those prayers automatically become a part of the *Congressional Record.* However, in 1970 the Supreme Court let stand a lower court ruling declaring it unconstitutional for students to read the prayers contained in the Congressional Record to a group of fellow students who voluntarily assembled before school to listen to the reading of those prayers![33]

A year later the Supreme Court outlawed the voluntary reading of a chapter of the Bible by students at the beginning of each school day. In a highly unusual move, the Court, which usually cites legal precedents for its rulings, instead chose to cite "expert" testimony from a psychologist who claimed that reading the Bible without any comment could be dangerous to the students' mental health: "If portions of the New Testament were read without explanation, they could be, and... had been, psychologically harmful to the [children]."[34]

Compare such an attitude about the Bible with that of Thomas Jefferson, the architect of the wall of separation: "I have always said, and always will say, that the studious perusal of the sacred volume [the Bible] will make us better citizens."[35]

Although the Supreme Court outlawed the reading of the Bible in public schools, it did not forbid the reading of every book about Jesus Christ. In 1985 a high-school student named Cassie Grove sought to have the book *A Learning Tree* removed from the school curriculum because of its offensive remarks to Christians such as ones that declared Jesus Christ to be a "poor white trash God" or "a long-legged white son-of-a-bitch."[36]

The Court ruled against Cassie Grove and allowed the book to remain part of the required curriculum. In other words, the Court declared it permissible to use a book in the public schools that refers to Jesus as a "son of a bitch," but you cannot read from the Book that declares Him to be the Son of God!

Significantly, the Court's decision directly contradicted an earlier Supreme Court opinion regarding blasphemy. One hundred and seventy years earlier in the case of *The People v. Ruggles* (1811), the Court considered similarly offensive remarks about Jesus but arrived at a completely different decision:

"Jesus Christ was a bastard, and his mother must be a whore."...
Such words...were an offense at common law.... It tends to corrupt the morals of the people, and to destroy good order. Such
offenses...are treated as affecting the essential interests of civil
society.[37]

In recent years the judiciary has not only sought to prohibit students from talking to or reading about God in schools, but they would
prefer that students refrain from thinking about Him as well. In 1967
a kindergarten teacher had her students recite the following poem:

We thank you for the flowers so sweet;
We thank you for the food we eat;
We thank you for the birds that sing;
We thank you for everything.[38]

The Supreme Court let stand a lower court ruling prohibiting the
poem, even though the poem does not contain the word *God.* As one
dissenting Supreme Court justice noted, the Court was now in the business of policing students' thoughts:

Thus we are asked as a court to prohibit, not only what these
children are saying, but also what...the children are thinking....
One who seeks to convert a child's supposed thought into a violation of the constitution of the United States is placing a meaning on that historic doctrine which would have surprised the
founding fathers.[39]

Surprised indeed! Can you imagine the response of George Washington, the acknowledged father of our nation, to such a ruling? On

October 3, 1789, Washington issued a proclamation establishing Thanksgiving as a national holiday to express our gratitude, not to some nameless deity, but to Almighty God:

> Whereas it is the duty of all nations to acknowledge the providence of Almighty God, to obey His will, to be grateful for His benefits, and humbly to implore His protection and favour...that we then may unite unto Him our sincere and humble thanks for His kind care and protection of the people of this country.[40]

Yet two hundred years later, the Supreme Court prohibited preschool children from reciting a poem that might cause them to even *think* about expressing gratitude to God!

Perhaps one of the most outlandish applications of the doctrine of separation of church and state occurred in 1980. Schools in the State of Kentucky had copies of the Ten Commandments posted in their hallways. Realize that no student was required to read the commandments, and no teacher was allowed to expound upon the meaning of the commandments. They were simply displayed on the wall: "Thou shalt not steal; thou shalt not bear false witness against thy neighbor; thou shalt not kill," and so on. In the case of *Stone v. Graham* (1980), the Supreme Court ruled that the posting of the Ten Commandments was unconstitutional. Why? If I told you, you would not believe me—so read the Court's reasoning for yourself:

> If the posted copies of the Ten Commandments are to have any effect at all, it will be to induce the schoolchildren to read, meditate upon, perhaps to venerate and obey, the Commandments.... This...is not a permissible state objective under the Establishment Clause [First Amendment].[41]

The Supreme Court was afraid that simply displaying a copy of the Ten Commandments might motivate students to "venerate and obey" the commandments. Heaven forbid that should happen!

When I read this ruling, I thought about another event that occurred in the hallway of a Kentucky school seventeen years after the Supreme Court's ruling. On the morning of December 1, 1997, a dozen students at Heath High School in Paducah, Kentucky, gathered to pray before classes, just as they did every day. As they closed their prayer time, a fourteen-year-old freshman approached the prayer group and, without any provocation, began shooting. Three students died and five others were seriously wounded in a hallway where, according to the Supreme Court, it was illegal to post the words "Thou shalt not kill."

The devastating consequences of purposefully removing any acknowledgment of God and His Word from public life are not limited to one high school in Kentucky. William Bennett, the former Secretary of Education under President Reagan, observed in a report titled *The Index of Leading Cultural Indicators* that during the same period of time (1960–1990) during which the judiciary worked overtime to separate our country from its strong Christian heritage, there was "a 560 percent increase in violent crime, a 419 percent increase in illegitimate births, a quadrupling in divorce rates,…and a drop of almost 80 points in SAT scores."[42] Today, an estimated 3 million teenagers are problem drinkers,[43] 4,000 children die each year as a result of gun violence,[44] and approximately 250,000 teenage girls have "legal" abortions each year.[45]

Just a coincidence? Not when you consider God's warning to the nation of Israel that is just as applicable to us today:

My people are destroyed for lack of knowledge.
Because you have rejected knowledge,

I also will reject you from being My priest.

Since you have forgotten the law of your God,

I also will forget your children. (Hosea 4:6)

God is no respecter of people or nations. The nation that reverences God and His Word will be blessed of God, and the nation that rejects God and His Word will be rejected by God. "Blessed is the nation whose God is the LORD" (Psalm 33:12).

Of course, such an idea is deemed politically incorrect in today's culture of diversity. Many have fooled themselves into thinking that religious pluralism (the worship of many gods) is the great strength of our nation. They applaud the courts' determined efforts to reverse 160 years of American history in which Christianity was elevated above every other "imposter religion," to use the terminology of the Supreme Court in 1892.

But "diversity" and "pluralism" are just euphemisms for what God calls "idolatry." God doesn't celebrate religious diversity, He condemns it. The first and greatest commandment of all was "You shall have no other gods before Me" (Exodus 20:3). When Israel was about to enter Canaan, a land filled with those who worshiped pagan deities, God commanded the Israelites to "put away the foreign gods which are in your midst" (Joshua 24:23) and warned them not to even mention the names of these other deities (Joshua 23:7). Tragically, Israel ignored God's commands and incurred His harshest judgments because of her tolerance for the worship of other gods.

Do you think God's opinion of idolatry has changed in the last three thousand years? Do you think Jehovah God is relieved that our nation no longer elevates Him and His Son Jesus Christ above other gods? "There is no one besides Me. I am the LORD, and there is no other" (Isaiah 45:6).

I decided to close this chapter not with a Bible verse or an observation from an evangelical Christian, but with the reflections of a man who could hardly be labeled a rabid fundamentalist. When I was growing up in the South during the 1950s and early 1960s, Earl Warren, the Chief Justice of the Supreme Court, was widely regarded as a "liberal" at best and frequently labeled as a "Communist pinko" by those who were opposed to civil rights for all Americans. But in 1954 Warren gave this assessment of our nation's Christian heritage:

> I believe no one can read the history of our country without realizing the Good Book and the Spirit of the Savior have from the beginning been our guiding geniuses…whether we look to the First Charter of Virginia, or to the Charter of New England, or to the Charter of Massachusetts Bay, or the Fundamental Orders of Connecticut. The same object is present; a Christian land governed by Christian principles. I believe the entire Bill of Rights came into being because of the knowledge our forefathers had of the Bible, and their belief in it; freedom of belief, of expression, of assembly, of petition, the dignity of the individual, the sanctity of the home, equal justice under the law, and the reservation of powers to the people. I like to believe we are living today in the spirit of the Christian religion. I like also to believe that as long as we do so, no great harm can come to our country.[46]

The nation that reverences God and His Word will be blessed of God; the nation that rejects God and His Word will be rejected by God. The choice is ours.

Becoming a Velvet-Covered Brick

So what's your new book about?" Bobby, a successful insurance salesman, asked me as we downed a cheeseburger together at our church's snack bar. That question always makes an author nervous, especially as he approaches the end of a yearlong process of writing in virtual solitude. Although the concept for the book has been thoroughly vetted by the publisher before the writing begins, no one really knows at that point whether the average book buyer will "bite" when the book is finally placed on the shelf. Here was a chance for me to engage in some rudimentary market research with a potential customer.

After explaining the concept of the book in a few sentences, I was pleasantly surprised by Bobby's response. "If ever there was a time for this kind of book, it's now," he assured me as, between bites, he lamented the condition of our culture and the lack of courage among Christians. "But may I offer you a word of advice?"

"Sure," I replied, not knowing what to expect next. He proceeded cautiously.

"Robert, you and I are a lot alike. We have strongly held convictions, and we can argue them persuasively. But somewhere in this book you need to remind your readers of a principle I learned from famed attorney Gerry Spence and use in my business every day."

"What's that?" I asked, wondering what advice a liberal attorney known mostly for his Western wardrobe and obnoxious personality could have for me.

"Spence says, 'To win an argument, you must empower the other party to continue the argument,'" Bobby replied.

I asked Bobby to explain what he meant.

"People like us who have strong personalities and rhetorical ability think that if we can silence our opponent, we've won the argument. But any married person knows that's not the case. If you are having a disagreement with your wife, it is easy through intimidation or insult to cause her to disengage from the discussion. But you haven't persuaded her of anything, except that you're a jerk."

I was beginning to get the point.

Bobby continued, "What you want to do is encourage the other party to continue the dialogue. The longer you continue the conversation, the better chance you have to eventually win him or her over to your point of view."

"But how do you do that?" I asked.

"You ask questions, you respect rather than denigrate their point of view, you listen—really listen—to them, and you demonstrate genuine concern for them. Remember, the goal is to keep the dialogue going with the other person, not to shut him or her down."

Unfortunately, silencing rather than influencing the opponent has been the tactic of too many Christians, including myself, when debating the issues we have discussed in this book. I thought about some of the heated exchanges I had engaged in on television and radio with a lesbian pastor, a leader of the ACLU, and a skilled attorney. I used my best one-line zingers, kept talking over my opponent, and tried to get the last word in before the commercial break. Of course, it made for entertaining television and won me accolades from friends and family members ("You really got them!"), but such theatrics did little to advance the argument. The goal is not winning the argument, but *winning over* the other person. Such an outcome cannot be achieved by rational arguments, research, or rhetoric alone. It takes something more. And in this last chapter, I want us to discover what that "something more" is.

As Bobby elaborated on Gerry Spence's comment about "empowering the other party to continue the dialogue," I thought about Someone Who modeled that principle so masterfully that He not only won the argument, but He also won over the other party without ever compromising His belief in absolute truth. Jesus's encounter with the Samaritan woman, recorded in John 4, illustrates how to be "hard" in your beliefs but "soft" with people. Jesus was the perfect example of what we all need to become if we are going to win over those who hold opposing points of view: a velvet-covered brick.

Long before anyone ever heard of Gerry Spence, Jesus Christ demonstrated four principles for winning people instead of just winning arguments.

1. Engage with those who hold opposing points of view. I love the story about the woman who was confiding to her next-door neighbor about her husband: "George is driving me crazy with his obsession with fishing. Every day after work he comes home, runs to the bathroom, puts on his waders, hops in the bathtub, and starts fishing out of the commode."

"That's terrible," the neighbor responded. "Have you taken him to a psychiatrist?"

"No," the woman sighed, "I've been too busy cleaning fish."

Here's a simple truth. If you want to catch fish, you have to go where the fish are. Jesus understood that principle. As an avid Fisherman of men and women, Jesus went where the people were. In the opening verses of John 4, the apostle recorded, "[Jesus] left Judea and went away again into Galilee. And He had to pass through Samaria" (verses 3-4).

Had to pass through Samaria? Why? There were certainly other routes Jesus could have taken from Judea (located in southern Palestine) to the northern region of Galilee. But Jesus "had to pass through Samaria" because He had a divine appointment with a potential new "catch" for His kingdom. Instead of hanging out in a monastery with His disciples, Jesus was regularly hitting the pavement recruiting new converts. During the three brief years He spent here on earth, His goal was not isolation, but influence. And He urged us to adopt the same mind-set as well: "You are the salt of the earth; but if the salt has become tasteless, how can it be made salty again?… You are the light of the world. A city set on a hill cannot be hidden" (Matthew 5:13-14).

In Jesus's day salt was a highly valued commodity used not only to add flavor to food but also to preserve the food in the days when refrigeration was unavailable. However, for salt to perform its job, it had to come into contact with the food. It could not stay on the shelf or in the shaker; it had to rub up against and penetrate the meat it was flavoring and preserving. At the same time it was imperative that the salt not be diluted or it would become worthless and be thrown away.

How are we to respond to the decaying culture in which we live? Some Christians so *identify* with world that they lose their "saltiness" and become worthless to God's kingdom. Other Christians, fearful of contamination by the culture, go to the opposite extreme and *isolate* themselves from unbelievers. They huddle together in churches, Christian schools, and fellowship groups, hoping to insulate themselves against any contact with unbelievers that might corrupt them.

But Jesus discourages us from either identifying with or isolating ourselves from our culture. Instead, He urges us to *influence* our world. And we can do that only when we come into contact with unbelievers—up close and personal.

Jesus used another metaphor to illustrate that truth. For light to dispel the darkness, it must first collide with the darkness. For example, when you enter a dark garage, a flashlight in your pocket does you little good. It makes no sense to say, "I will keep my flashlight hidden so I won't offend the darkness." For darkness to be removed, it must come in contact with the light! That is what Jesus meant when He said, "You are the light of the world. A city set on a hill cannot be hidden; nor does anyone light a lamp and put it under a basket, but on a lampstand, and it gives light to all who are in the house" (Matthew 5:14-15).

The reason God has placed you in a specific family, neighborhood, school, company, or seat on an airplane is so that you might influence others with the light of God's truth. But you can never influence people for Christ without first coming in contact with them!

In preparation for special evangelistic services we have at our church, I often ask our church members to fill out a little card with the heading "Five Most Wanted" on which they list five non-Christians they will pray for and invite to the services. I am always amazed by how many people have difficulty completing the card! By the way, could you fill one out? Can you name five non-Christians you are praying for and seeking to influence for God?

At the beginning of my freshman year in high school, my English teacher, who was a Christian, asked if I would stay after school for a moment to talk with her. She said, "Robert, I believe there is a reason God has placed you in this school. He wants you to be a witness for Him. I would like to challenge you to list the names of five non-Christian students you know, commit to praying for their salvation, and make an appointment with them sometime this year to share the gospel with them."

I accepted the challenge and began to pray for those opportunities. The first boy on my list was Nick. He was what we called in those days a "hood," complete with leather jacket, cigarettes, and a Bronx accent (which certainly stood out in Texas). He looked as if he had stepped right out of Central Casting for an audition in *West Side Story*. One day I screwed up my courage and asked Nick if I could talk with him after classes. Amazingly he agreed, and on that fall afternoon in an empty classroom at West Junior High School, I shared with him *The Four Spiritual Laws* evangelistic booklet. "Is there anything that would keep you from wanting to trust in Christ as your Savior?" I concluded.

Even more surprisingly, he replied, "No, I would like to do that." And I had the privilege of leading someone to Christ for the first time in my life.

Nine months later Nick died of a brain tumor, and I understood for the first time the urgency of the mission Christ has entrusted to every Christian. During that school year of 1970–1971, I shared the gospel with everyone on my list, and each of them became a believer, including a girl on that list who would later become my wife.

Let me point out that if I had attended a Christian school or had been homeschooled, I might not have had that opportunity. But along with that Christian teacher, I had parents who, early in my life, instilled in me a sense of mission—not just by their words—but by their example. Some of my earliest memories are of my parents, now in heaven, inviting non-Christian neighbors over for dinner and then listening to an evangelistic tape or watching a Billy Graham crusade on television.

When I was ten years old, my mother, who was a journalism teacher in a public school, was supposed to take two of her Jewish students to an all-day conference one Saturday. She asked me to go with them so that at a predetermined time during the one-hour car trip, I could innocently ask, "Mom, how can a person go to heaven when he dies?"

Right on cue, I blurted out the question, and the two girls rolled their eyes as my mom launched into her well-rehearsed answer. My mom's method may have been flawed, but her motive was right! To influence unbelievers we must first engage with them rather than isolate ourselves from them.

2. Listen to other people's stories. The way we influence others, however, is not by cornering them and then dumping our "stuff" on them as my well-intentioned mom tried to do (and I have done as well). The late Paul Little vividly described the futility of such an approach:

I wish I'd learned this lesson about communicating with people sooner. About once every six months the pressure to witness used to reach explosive heights inside me. Not knowing any better, I would suddenly lunge at someone and spout all my verses with a sort of glazed stare in my eye. I honestly didn't expect any response. As soon as my victim indicated lack of interest, I'd begin to edge away from him with a sigh of relief and the consoling thought, "All that will live godly in Christ Jesus shall suffer persecution" (II Timothy 3:12). Duty done, I'd draw back into my martyr's shell for another six months' hibernation, until the internal pressure again became intolerable and drove me out. It really shocked me when I finally realized that I, not the cross, was offending people. My inept, unwittingly rude, even stupid approach to them was responsible for their rejection of me and the gospel message.[1]

Instead of unloading our spiritual dump truck of arguments and answers to unasked questions, we need to carefully listen to the person we are trying to influence. Bobby, my insurance salesman friend, told me, "A good salesman learns to listen—really listen—to a potential customer." Why? "By listening you learn his interests, his needs, and his potential objections to your product."

It is significant that Jesus did not begin His discussion with the Samaritan woman by asking, "If you were to stand before God and He were to ask you, 'Why should I let you into my kingdom?' what would you say?" Instead, He began with a topic of interest to her: water. She had a need for water, and from her felt need, Jesus was able to offer her something much better that would satisfy her spiritual thirst:

> Jesus answered and said to her, "Everyone who drinks of this
> water will thirst again; but whoever drinks of the water that I
> will give him shall never thirst; but the water that I will give him
> will become in him a well of water springing up to eternal life."
> (John 4:13-14)

The other day I was on my way to Denver to lead a conference on Bible prophecy. I was mad at myself for forgetting to cancel my request for an automatic upgrade to first class, thereby wasting some of my accumulated miles. But as I began to converse with my seatmate, I understood that my forgetfulness was no accident. I was in seat 4A for a reason.

The gentleman next to me was a Jewish stockbroker. I spent the majority of the time listening to his theories about the market and his political views about the president. As the time for landing grew closer, I started to feel Paul Little's pressure building inside me to "unload" the gospel on him before the wheels touched down.

But with this recently completed chapter fresh in my mind, I relaxed and just listened. The stockbroker talked about his synagogue's fund-raising efforts and his plans to leave a trust fund for its support: "That is the only part of me that will live on after I die."

Then he told me of a recent brain tumor and his genuine fear of death. Those two comments gave me a brief opportunity to share a few words about the possibility of life after death. Had I spoken prematurely, he would undoubtedly have been offended and ended the conversation. But by listening, I gained some insight into his needs and earned the right to continue our discussion through correspondence.

Everyone has a story to tell, and we must give people a chance to tell their stories if we want to influence them. The reason someone might object to the idea that "homosexuality is a perversion" might be because a family member is dying of AIDS. A woman who bristles at the notion of her husband being the head of the family might be living with an abusive mate. A parent who has lost a child through disease or accident may understandably be offended by the idea that "God is responsible for suffering." Everyone has a story to tell, and we must be willing to listen—really listen—to that story without judging.

3. Distinguish between major and minor issues. Some readers of this book might wonder why I did not place the chapter on hell at the beginning, given the title of the book. The reason is simple. Belief in a literal hell is not necessary for salvation. Nor must a person accept that homosexuality is a perversion, that evolution is a myth, or that the husband is the head of the family to be welcomed into God's presence. The first politically incorrect truth we discussed concerning the exclusivity of the gospel message is the *only* essential belief a person must embrace to receive eternal life.

That doesn't mean we don't deem the other beliefs to be important; instead, we put them in perspective just as Jesus did. Even though the Samaritan woman was living in an immoral relationship, Jesus did not argue the merits of sexual abstinence with her. When she attempted to sidetrack Jesus with a theological argument concerning the proper temple in which to worship God, Jesus ignored the question and focused on a more important issue: the woman's personal relationship with God.

Similarly, we should not expect people to accept the truths we have discussed in this book without their first embracing the One who called Himself the Truth.

4. Reflect the love of Christ. A debater's goal is to win the argument. A disciple's goal is to win the person. I've discovered the hard way that it is possible to win the battle of words but lose the war over a person's soul by being unnecessarily harsh. Many non-Christians have rejected the gospel not because of the offense of the Cross, but because of the offensiveness of Christians. Gandhi once observed, "I might be persuaded to become a Christian...if I ever met one."

The Samaritan woman was ultimately drawn not to dogma, but to a Person. When she ran into the city to tell people what had happened to her, she did not shout, "Come and listen to these *ideas* that have changed my mind," but "Come, see a *Man* who has changed my life!" (John 4:29, author's paraphrase). Our ultimate objective is not to attract people to our ideas, but to our Savior.

Arthur Burns was a Washington power broker who served as chairman of the Federal Reserve, as ambassador to West Germany, and in other prominent positions from the 1960s through the 1980s. He was a counselor and confidant to a number of U.S. presidents during his career. Arthur Burns was also Jewish.

That is why his regular attendance at a weekly Bible study and prayer meeting at the White House in the 1970s was a surprise to many.

Although he was warmly welcomed, different members of the group who took turns leading the meetings never called on him to pray.

One week, however, a newcomer leading the group asked Arthur Burns to close in prayer. The other members shot a glance at one another, wondering how Burns would respond to this awkward situation. Burns never hesitated. Instead, he joined hands with the others in the group, bowed his head, and prayed, "Lord, I pray that you would bring Jews to know Jesus Christ. I pray that you would bring Muslims to know Jesus Christ. Finally, Lord, I pray that you would bring Christians to know Jesus Christ. Amen."[2]

The more we know—and reflect—the loving compassion of Jesus Christ, the more we will influence others to say no to hell and yes to heaven.

A discussion guide on the topics covered in *Hell? Yes!*
is available free of charge at *www.waterbrookpress.com.*

Notes

Wimp-Free Christianity

1. Michael Willhoite, *Daddy's Roommate* (Boston: Alyson Publications, 1990), 26.
2. Willhoite, *Daddy's Roommate,* 6.
3. Letter to the editor, *Times Record News,* May 20, 1998.
4. Barna Research Online, "Americans Are Most Likely to Base Truth on Feelings," February 12, 2002. Found at www.barna.org. Copyright © 2002 Barna Research Group, Ltd. Used by permission. All rights reserved.
5. Barna Research Online, "Americans Are Most Likely." Used by permission. All rights reserved.
6. George Barna, "Morality and the Church," (2002) videotape; quoted in Barna Research Online, "Americans Are Most Likely."
7. Allan Bloom, *The Closing of the American Mind* (New York: Simon & Schuster, 1987), 26.
8. Carson Holloway, "From Playboy to Pedophilia: How Adult Sexual Liberation Leads to Children's Sexual Exploitation," lecture given at Family Research Council symposium on July 10, 2002. Found at www.frc.org/get.cfm?i=WT02G1&f=AR01K4.
9. Holloway, "From Playboy to Pedophilia."
10. *Ashcroft v. Free Speech Coalition,* no. 00-795, 8-10. In Holloway, "From Playboy to Pedophilia."
11. Laura Schlessinger, quoted in "Sexual-Abuse Study Disgusts Concerned Dad," *Dallas Morning News,* April 15, 1999.

12. Sören Andersson, quoted in Gregory Tomlin, "A Wave of Contempt for God's Word," *Southwestern News* (Winter 2003). Found at www.swbts.edu/happenings/southwesternnews/pdf/winter2003/lastword.pdf.

13. Annalie Enochson, *Catholic World News* (June 2003), quoted in Tomlin, "A Wave of Contempt."

14. Tomlin, "A Wave of Contempt."

15. Judge Samuel B. Kent, quoted in Brannon Howse, "The People and Agenda of Multicultural Education," *Understanding the Times* (January 1997): 3; Josh McDowell and Bob Hostetler, *The New Tolerance: How a Cultural Movement Threatens to Destroy You* (Wheaton, IL: Tyndale, 1998), 53.

16. Barna, "Morality and the Church," in Barna Research Online, "Americans Are Most Likely."

17. Leslie Armour, quoted in Bob Harvey, "Wanted: Old Fashioned Virtue," *Montreal Gazette* (19 February 1995); McDowell, *The New Tolerance,* 43.

18. Dr. Frederick W. Hill, quoted in Stephen Bates, "Religious Diversity and the Schools," *The American Enterprise* 4, no. 5 (September/October 1993): 19; McDowell, *The New Tolerance,* 43.

19. Bob Woodward, *Bush at War: Inside the Bush White House* (New York: Simon & Schuster, 2002), 131.

20. R. C. Sproul, quoted in Scott Scruggs, "Truth or Tolerance?" Probe Ministries International (1996). Found at www.probe.org/docs/truthtol.html.

21. William Watkins, *The New Absolutes: How They Are Being Imposed on Us—How They Are Eroding Our Moral Landscape* (Minneapolis, MN: Bethany House, 1996), 240.

Chapter 1: Every Other Religion Is Wrong

1. Dr. Al Mohler, Michael Brown, and Rabbi Schmuley Boteach, interview by Phil Donahue, *Donahue,* MSNBC, August 20, 2002. Transcript found at www.msnbc.com/news/797116.asp.

2. Scott Scruggs, "Truth or Tolerance?" Probe Ministries International (1996). Found at www.probe.org/docs/truthtol.html.

3. Thomas A. Helmbock, "Insights on Tolerance," *Cross and Crescent* (Summer 1996): 2. Quoted in Josh McDowell and Bob Hostetler, *The New Tolerance: How a Cultural Movement Threatens to Destroy You* (Wheaton, IL: Tyndale, 1998), 19.

4. Judge Danny Boggs, quoted in Stephen Bates, "Religious Diversity and the Schools," *The American Enterprise* 4, no. 5 (September/October 1993): 18; McDowell, *The New Tolerance,* 19.

5. Rabbi Boteach, interview by Larry King, *Larry King Live,* January 12, 2000. Found at www.cnn.com/TRANSCRIPTS/0001/12/lkl.00.html.

6. Transcript of remarks delivered by former president William Jefferson Clinton at Georgetown University, November 7, 2001. Found at www.georgetown.edu/admin/publicaffairs/protocol_events/events/clinton_glf110701.htm.

7. Gene Edward Veith Jr., *Postmodern Times* (Wheaton, IL: Crossway Books, 1994), 16. In Scruggs, "Truth or Tolerance?"

8. Charles Templeton, *Farewell to God* (Toronto: McClelland and Stewart, 1996), 27.

9. James M. Boice, *Romans,* vol. 1 (Grand Rapids: Baker, 1991), 173.

10. Susan Cyre, "Fallout Escalates over 'Goddess' Sophia Worship," *Christianity Today* (4 April 1994): 74.

11. Cyre, "Fallout," 74.

12. Ravi Zacharias, *Jesus Among Other Gods: The Absolute Claims of the Christian Message* (Nashville: Word, 2000), 7.

13. Clark H. Pinnock, *A Wideness in God's Mercy: The Finality of Jesus Christ in a World of Religions* (Grand Rapids: Zondervan, 1992), 151-52.

14. Phil Donahue, *Donahue,* August 20, 2002. Found at www.msnbc.com/news/797116.asp.

15. Franklin Graham, *The Name* (Nashville: Nelson, 2002), 33.

16. Account adapted from Jerome Greer Chandler, *Fire and Rain: A Tragedy in American Aviation* (Austin, TX: Texas Monthly Press, 1986).

Chapter 2: God Is Ultimately Responsible for Suffering

1. Evan Thomas, "Four Lives: Their Faith and Fears," *Newsweek* (9 September 2002): 42.

2. Joan Glick, quoted in Jere Longman, *Among the Heroes: United Flight 93 and the Passengers and Crew Who Fought Back* (New York: HarperCollins, 2002), 249.

3. John Stott, *The Cross of Christ* (Downers Grove, IL: InterVarsity, 1986), 311.

4. The OmniPoll, conducted by Barna Research Group, January 1999, quoted in Lee Strobel, *The Case for Faith: A Journalist Investigates the Toughest Objections to Christianity* (Grand Rapids: Zondervan, 2000), 29.

5. John G. Stackhouse Jr., "There Is an Answer to Evil," *Christianity Today* 28, no. 8 (18 May 1984): 40.

6. Bob and Gretchen Passantino, "If God Is Good, Why Is There So Much Suffering in the World?" (Costa Mesa, CA: Answers in Action, 1997). Found on answers.com/apologetics/suffering.html.

7. Ravi Zacharias, *Jesus Among Other Gods: The Absolute Claims of the Christian Message* (Nashville: Word, 2000), 113.

8. Ted Turner, quoted in Kurt De Haan, "Why Would a Good God Allow Suffering" (Grand Rapids: RBC Ministries, 1990). Found at www.gospelcom.net/rbc/ds/q0106/q0106.html.

9. Harold S. Kushner, *When Bad Things Happen to Good People* (New York: HarperCollins, 1981), 43-44.

10. Kushner, *When Bad Things Happen to Good People,* 148.

11. Elie Wiesel, quoted in Yancey, *Disappointment with God,* 208.

12. Erwin Lutzer, *Ten Lies About God and How You May Already Be Deceived* (Nashville: Word, 2000), 99.

13. Kushner, *When Bad Things Happen,* 139-40.

14. John Sanders and Chris Hall, "Does God Know Your Next Move?" *Christianity Today* 45, no. 7 (21 May 2001): 38.

15. Sanders and Hall, "Does God Know Your Next Move?" 38.

16. A. W. Tozer, *The Knowledge of the Holy* (San Francisco: Harper & Row, 1961), 1.

17. Dorothy L. Sayers, "The Greatest Drama Ever Staged," *The Poetry of Search and the Poetry of Statement* (London: Victor Gollancz, 1963). Found at www.goodnewsmag.org/magazine/6NovDec/nd02sayers.htm.

18. Steve Farrar, *Gettin' There: How a Man Finds His Way on the Trail of Life* (Sisters, OR: Multnomah, 2001), 47.

19. Max Lucado, *In the Eye of the Storm: A Day in the Life of Jesus* (Waco, TX: Word, 1991), 239.

20. Adapted from Strobel, *The Case for Faith,* 32.

21. C. S. Lewis, *Mere Christianity* (New York: Macmillan, 1952), 173.

22. Bryan Chapell, "Jesus Wept," *Preaching Today,* no. 229A (2002), audiotape transcript. Found at www.preachingtoday.com.

Chapter 3: God Sends Good People to Hell

1. The sermon "Sinners in the Hands of an Angry God" was preached by Jonathan Edwards at Enfield, Connecticut, on July 8, 1741. Found at www.jonathanedwards.com/sermons/ Warnings/sinners.htm.

2. Robert G. Ingersoll, quoted in Carl G. Johnson, *Hell, You Say!* (Newtown, PA: Timothy Books, 1974), vii.

3. Bertrand Russell, *Why I Am Not a Christian and Other Essays on Religion and Related Subjects* (New York: Simon & Schuster, 1957), 17.

4. "The IEA/Roper Center Theology Faculty Survey," *This World* 2 (1982): 50. In Jerry L. Walls, *Hell: The Logic of Damnation* (Notre Dame, IN: University of Notre Dame Press, 1993), 3.

5. James Davison Hunter, *Evangelicalism: The Coming Generation* (Chicago: University of Chicago Press, 1987), 38. In Larry Dixon, *The Other Side of the Good News* (Wheaton, IL: Victor Books, 1992), 11-12.

6. 1990 Gallup Poll, cited in "Hell's Sober Comeback," *U.S. News and World Report* (25 March 1991): 56; Walls, *Hell,* 3; Dixon, *The Other Side,* 11.

7. Pope John Paul II, "Hell Is the State of Those Who Reject God," *L'Osservatore Romano* (28 July 1999): 7. Found at www.solt3.org/purgatory2.htm.

8. Douglas Groothuis, quoted in Jeffery L. Sheler, "Hell Hath No Fury," *U.S. News & World Report* 128, no. 4 (31 January 2000), 46. Found at www.geocities.com/Paris/Cathedral/6070/ hell.html.

9. Sheler, "Hell Hath No Fury," 45. Found at www.geocities
    .com/Paris/Cathedral/6070/hell.html.

10. Jack MacArthur, *Exploring in the Next World* (Minneapolis:
    Dimension Books, 1967), 91. Quoted in Billy Graham, *Facing
    Death and the Life After* (Waco, TX: Word, 1987), 36.

11. R. Albert Mohler, quoted in Sheler, "Hell Hath No Fury,"
    45. Found at www.geocities.com/Paris/Cathedral/6070/
    hell.html.

12. Clark H. Pinnock, "The Destruction of the Finally Impenitent,"
    Criswell Theological Review 4, no. 2 (Spring 1990): 246-47.
    Quoted in Sheler, "Hell Hath No Fury," 50. Found at
    www.geocities.com/Paris/Cathedral/6070/hell.html.

13. James Hammond, quoted in John Ortberg, *The Life You've
    Always Wanted* (Grand Rapids: Zondervan, 2002), 125.

14. D. A. Carson, quoted in Lee Strobel, *The Case for Christ: A Jour-
    nalist's Personal Investigation of the Evidence for Jesus* (Grand
    Rapids: Zondervan, 2000), 222.

15. Based on Mark Littleton's illustration in "That Horrible Doc-
    trine," *Discipleship Journal,* no. 34 (1 July 1986): 13-15.

16. Sir Norman Anderson, *Christianity and World Religions: The
    Challenge of Pluralism* (Downers Grove, IL: InterVarsity, 1984),
    153. Found at www.gospelcom.net/rbc/ds/q1002.

17. J. I. Packer, "Hell's Final Enigma," *Christianity Today* 46, no. 5
    (22 April 2002): 84.

18. Larry Dixon, "Whatever Happened to Hell?" *Moody Monthly*
    93, no. 10 (June 1993): 29.

19. John H. Gerstner, "The Terror of the Lord," quoted in Dixon,
    "Whatever Happened to Hell?"

20. Martin Marty, quoted in "Hell's Sober Comeback," *U.S. News
    and World Report* (25 March 1991): 56; Donald L. Norbie, "Is

There an Eternal Hell?" Found at www.biblefollowship.org/
OnlineLibrary/Hell/IsThereAnEternalHell.html.

Chapter 4: Homosexuality Is a Perversion

1. Marshall Kirk and Hunter Madsen, *After the Ball: How America Will Conquer Its Fear and Hatred of Gays in the 1990s* (New York: Penquin, 1989), in Charles W. Socarides, "How America Went Gay" *America* (18 November 1995). Found at www.leaderu.com/jhs/socarides.html.

2. Kirk and Madsen, *After the Ball,* 148-50.

3. Kirk and Madsen, *After the Ball,* 150-53.

4. Kirk and Madsen, *After the Ball,* 153.

5. "The Homosexual in America," *Time* 87, no. 3 (21 January 1966): 41.

6. Socarides, "How America Went Gay."

7. Lynn Vincent, "The Liberal Future?" *World* 17, no. 3 (31 August 2002): 16. Found at www.worldmag.com/world/issue/08-31-02/cover_1.asp.

8. Pete Winn, "Bush Backs Marriage-Protection Amendment" (24 February 2004). Found at www.family.org/cforum/feature/a0030929.cfm.

9. Associated Press, "Rosie O'Donnell to Marry Girlfriend in San Francisco" (26 February 2004). Found at www.cnn.com/2004/SHOWBIZ/TV/02/26/odonnell.ap/index.html.

10. Thomas E. Schmidt, *Straight and Narrow? Compassion and Clarity in the Homosexuality Debate* (Downers Grove, IL: InterVarsity, 1995), 88-89.

11. Simon LeVay, "A Difference in the Hypothalamic Structure Between Heterosexual and Homosexual Men," *Science*

253 (30 August 1991): 1034-37. In Joe Dallas, "Responding to Pro-Gay Theology." Found at www.leaderu.com/jhs/ dallas.html.

12. "Sexual Disorientation: Faulty Research in the Homosexual Debate," *Family* (28 October 1992): 4. In Dallas, "Responding to Pro-Gay Theology." Found at www.leaderu.com/jhs/ dallas.html.

13. Dallas, "Responding to Pro-Gay Theology." Found at www .leaderu.com/jhs/dallas.html.

14. "Gay Genes Revisited," *Scientific American* (November 1995): 26. In Dallas, "Responding to Pro-Gay Theology." Found at www.leaderu.com/jhs/dallas.html.

15. Dr. Anne Fausto-Sterling, quoted in Christine Gorman, "Are Gay Men Born That Way?" *Time* (9 September 1991): 52.

16. "Is This Child Gay," *Newsweek* (9 September 1991): 52. In Dallas, "Responding to Pro-Gay Theology." Found at www .leaderu.com/jhs/dallas.html.

17. "A Genetic Study of Male Sexual Orientation," *Archives of General Psychiatry* 48 (1991): 1089-96; J. M. Bailey et al., "Heritable Factors Influence Sexual Orientation in Women," *Archives of General Psychiatry* 50 (March 1993): 217-23. In Schmidt, *Straight and Narrow?* Found at www.gospelcom.net/ivpress/ title/exc/1858-7.php.

18. Schmidt, *Straight and Narrow?* Found at www.gospelcom.net/ ivpress/title/exc/1858-7.php.

19. Schmidt, *Straight and Narrow?* Found at www.gospelcom.net/ ivpress/title/exc/1858-7.php.

20. Dallas, "Responding to Pro-Gay Theology." Found at www .leaderu.com/jhs/dallas.html.

21. Dallas, "Responding to Pro-Gay Theology." Found at www .leaderu.com/jhs/dallas.html.

22. Schmidt, *Straight and Narrow?* Found at www.gospelcom.net/ ivpress/title/exc/1858-7.php.

23. D. H. Hamer et al., "A Linkage Between DNA Markers on the X Chromosome and Male Sexual Orientation," *Science* 261, no. 5119 (July 1993): 321-27. In Dr. Jeffrey Satinover, "The Gay Gene," *Focus on the Family* (1999). Found at www.family.org.

24. Dallas, "Responding to Pro-Gay Theology." Found at www .leaderu.com/jhs/dallas.html.

25. From A. Fausto-Sterling and E. Balaban, "Genetics and Male Sexual Orientation," *Science* 261 (3 September 1993), in Schmidt, *Straight and Narrow?* Found at www.gospelcom .net/ivpress/title/exc/1858-7.php.

26. William Byne and Bruce Parsons, "Human Sexual Orientation: The Biologic Theories Reappraised," *Archives of General Psychiatry* 50, no. 3 (March 1993). Found at http://archpsyc.ama-assn .org/cgi.

27. Dr. Joe McIlhaney, in J. Budziszewski, "TV & Film: Debating Homosexuality," *World* 14, no. 3 (23 January, 1999). Found at www.worldmag.com/world/issue/01-23-99/cultural_3.asp.

28. Alan P. Bell and Martin S. Weinberg, *Homosexualities: A Study of Diversity Among Men and Women* (New York: Simon & Schuster, 1978), in Alan P. Medinger, "An Urgent Message of Warning to Gay Men: The Safe Sex Illusion" (1978). Found at www.exodus northamerica.org/infocenter/libraryarticles/a0000686.html.

29. L. McKusick et al., "Aids and Sexual Behaviors Reported by Gay Men in San Francisco," *American Journal of Public Health* 75 (December 1985): 493-96. In Paul Cameron, PhD, "Medical

Consequences of What Homosexuals Do" (1999). Found at www.familyresearchinst.org/FRI_EduPamphlet3.html.

30. Paul Cameron, PhD, "Medical Consequences of What Homosexuals Do." Found at www.familyresearchinst.org/ FRI_EduPamphlet3.html.

31. Cameron, "Medical Consequences." Found at www.family researchinst.org/FRI_EduPamphlet3.html.

32. Centers for Disease Control and Prevention, *HIV/AIDS Fact Sheet: Need for Sustained HIV Prevention Among Men Who Have Sex with Men* (August 1999), in Mike Haley, *Straight Answers: Exposing the Myths and Facts About Homosexuality* (Colorado Springs: Focus on the Family, 2001), 13.

33. Mark E. Pietrzyk, "Queer Science," *The New Republic* (3 October 1994). Found at www.indegayforum.org/authors/pietrzyk/ pietrzyk53.html.

34. Family Research Council, "Sexual Disorientation: Faulty Research in the Homosexual Debate" (June 1992), in Alan P. Medinger, "Great Myths About Homosexuality." Found at www.exodus-international.org/library_Society_06.shtml.

35. Robert J. Kus, "Alcoholics and Gay American Men," *Journal of Homosexuality* 114, no. 2 (1987), in Medinger, "Great Myths About Homosexuality." Found at www.exodus-international .org/library_Society_06.shtml.

36. Bell and Weinberg, *Homosexualities,* in Medinger, "Great Myths About Homosexuality." Found at www.exodus-international .org/library_Society_06.shtml.

37. Paul Cameron, W. Playfair, and S. Wellum, "The Lifespan of Homosexuals." Paper presented at the Eastern Psychological Association Convention on April 17, 1993. In Cameron,

"Medical Consequences." Found at www.familyresearchinst.org/FRI_EduPamphlet3.html.

38. Alfred Kinsey, *Sexual Behavior in the Human Male* (Philadelphia: Saunders Press: 1948), ix, 651.

39. Judith A. Reisman and Edward W. Eichel, *Kinsey, Sex and Fraud: The Indoctrination of a People* (Lafayette, LA: Lochinvar/Huntington House, 1990), 9.

40. *USA Today* (15 April 1993), in Dallas, "Responding to Pro-Gay Theology." Found at www.leaderu.com/jhs/dallas.html.

41. Jill Harris, ACT-Up, quoted in the movie *Gay Rights, Special Rights* (Jeremiah Films, 1993), quoted in Haley, *Straight Answers,* 7.

42. Theo Sandfort, "Pedophilia and the Gay Movement," *The Journal of Homosexuality* (1987), in Paul Cameron, PhD, "Child Molestation and Homosexuality," (1999). Found at www.familyresearchinst.org/FRI_EduPamphlet2.html.

43. *Stonewall Union Reports* (February 1991), in Cameron, "Child Molestation." Found at www.familyresearchinst.org/FRI_EduPamphlet2.html.

44. Bell and Weinberg, *Homosexualities;* S. K. Hammersmith, *Sexual Preference: Statistical Appendix* (Bloomington, IN: Indiana University Press, 1981), in Dr. Paul Cameron, "Born WHAT Way?" (1999). Found at www.familyreseachinst.org.

45. Irving Bieber, *Homosexuality: A Psychoanalytic Study* (New York: Basic Books, 1962), 319.

46. Ruben Fine, *Psychoanalytic Theory, Male and Female Homosexuality: Psychological Approaches* (New York: Hemisphere, 1987), 84-86. Quoted in Dallas, "Responding to Pro-Gay Theology." Found at www.leaderu.com/jhs/dallas.html.

Chapter 5: Husbands Are to Be the Leaders of Their Families

1. Jack and Judith Balswick, "Adam and Eve in America," *Christianity Today* (16 July 1990): 17-18. Found at www.christianity today.com/ct/2002/109/51.0.html.

2. Agnieszka Tennant, "Adam and Eve in the 21st Century," *Christianity Today* 46, no. 3 (11 March 2002): 61. Found at www.christianitytoday.com/ct/2002/003/40.61.html.

3. Wayne Grudem, quoted in Agnieszka Tennant, "Nuptial Agreements," *Christianity Today* 46, no. 3 (11 March 2002): 59-60. Found at www.christianitytoday.com/ct/2002/003/4.58.html.

4. Aristotle, *On the Generation of Animals,* quoted in Simone de Beauvoir, *The Second Sex,* trans. H. M. Parshley (New York: Vintage, Random House, 1974), introduction.

5. U.S. Army Field Manual, "Physical Fitness Training" fm. 21-20 (1 October 1998). Found at www.adtdl.army.mil/cgi-bin/atdl.dll/query/info/FM+21-20.

6. A. Duane Litfin, "A Biblical View of the Marital Roles: Seeking a Balance," *Bibliotheca Sacra* 133, no. 532 (October–December 1976): 336-37.

7. Wayne Grudem, "Does *kephale* ('Head') Mean 'Source' or 'Authority Over' in Greek Literature? A Survey of 2,336 Examples" *Trinity Journal* 6 NS (1985): 38-59. In Wayne Grudem and John Piper, *Recovering Biblical Manhood & Womanhood: A Response to Evangelical Feminism* (Wheaton, IL: Crossway, 2004), appendix. Found at www.leaderu.com/orgs/cbmw/rbmw/appendix1a.html.

8. Grudem, "Does *kephale* ('Head') Mean 'Source,' " in Grudem and Piper, *Recovering Biblical Manhood.* Found at www.leaderu.com/orgs/cbmw/rbmw/appendix1a.html.

9. John Eldredge, *Wild at Heart* (Nashville: Nelson, 2001), 115.

10. Steve Farrar, *Gettin' There* (Sisters, OR: Multnomah, 2001), 137.

11. James Montgomery Boice, *Genesis,* vol. 1 (Grand Rapids: Zondervan, 1982), 179.

12. Harold S. Kushner, *Living a Life That Matters* (New York: Knopf, 2001), 32.

13. Litfin, "A Biblical View of Marital Roles," 336.

14. Jim M. Alsdurf, "Wife Abuse and the Church: The Response of Pastors," *Response to the Victimization of Women and Children* 8, no. 1 (Winter 1985): 9-11. In J. Lee Grady. "Control Freaks and the Women Who Love Them," *New Man* 8, no. 1 (January–February 2001): 41.

15. Grady, "Control Freaks," 40.

16. John Stott, *God's New Society: The Message of Ephesians* (Downers Grove, IL: InterVarsity, 1979), 218-19. Quoted in R. Kent Hughes, *Ephesians: The Mystery of the Body of Christ* (Wheaton, IL: Crossway, 1990). Found at www.cbmw.org/resources/articles/mystery_of_marriage1.php.

17. *HIS* (May 1978): 17. Quoted in John W. Alexander, "Headship in Marriage: Flip of a Coin?" *Christianity Today* 25, no. 4 (20 February 1981): 25.

18. Adapted from Steve Farrar, *Gettin' There,* 139-41.

Chapter 6: Evolution Is a Myth

1. Letter of protest from Robert Palazzo, PhD, and Paul Berg, PhD, sent to Governor Bill Graves of Kansas on August 26, 1999. Found at www.jscpp.org/Kansas.htm.

2. Maxine Singer, "Believing Is Not Understanding," *The Washington Post* (18 August 1999).

3. Zogby International, "American Values Poll," February 2000. Found at www.zogby.com/news/ReadNews.dbm?ID=199.

4. NOVA, *The Miracle of Life,* photographed by Lennart Nilsson (Boston: WGBH Educational Foundation, 1986), videotape. In Hank Hanegraaff, "Fat Chance: The Failure of Evolution to Account for the Miracle of Life" (1998). Found at www.equip .org/free/DC745.htm.

5. Jonathan Weiner, quoted in Nancy Pearcey, "We're Not in Kansas Anymore," *Christianity Today* 44, no. 6 (22 May 2000): 42. Found at www.christianitytoday.com/ct/2000/006/1.42.html.

6. Pearcey, "We're Not in Kansas." Found at www.christianity today.com/ct/2000/006/1.42.html.

7. Jerry Adler and John Carey, "Is Man a Subtle Accident?" *Newsweek* 96, no. 18 (3 November 1980): 54. Quoted in David B. Loughran, "Evolution: Fact or Fallacy?" (April 1996). Found at http://atschool.eduweb.co.uk/sbs777/vital/evolutio.html.

8. American National Association of Biology Teachers 1995 position statement, quoted in Phillip E. Johnson, *Defeating Darwinism by Opening Minds* (Downers Grove, IL: InterVarsity, 1997), 15.

9. Michael Bauman, ed., *Man and Creation: Perspectives on Science and Theology* (Hillsdale, MI: Hillsdale College Press, 1993). In Phillip E. Johnson, "What Is Darwinism? " *Christian Research Journal* (1997). Found at www.equip.org/free/DE382.htm.

10. Richard Lewontin, "Billions and Billions of Demons," *The New York Review of Books* (9 January 1997), 31. Quoted in Pearcey, "We're Not in Kansas." Found at www.christianitytoday.com/ct/ 2000/006/1.42.html.

11. Allan Sandage, quoted in George Johnson, "Science and Religion: Bridging the Great Divide," *The New York Times* (30 June 1998). Found at www.stephenjaygould/ctrl/news/file023.html.

12. James F. Coppedge, *Evolution: Possible or Impossible?* (Northridge, CA: Probability Research in Molecular Biology, 1993), 110, 114. In Hanegraaff, "Fat Chance." Found at www.equip.org/free/DC745.htm.

13. Michael J. Behe, "Experimental Support for Regarding Functional Classes of Proteins to Be Highly Isolated from Each Other," *The Weekly Standard* (7 June 1999). Found at www.arn.org/docs/behe/mb_smu1992.htm.

14. Coppedge, *Evolution?* 119-24. In Hanegraaff, "Fat Chance." Found at www.equip.org/free/DC745.htm.

15. Coppedge, *Evolution?* In Hanegraaff, "Fat Chance." Found at www.equip.org/free/DC745.htm.

16. Michael J. Behe, *Darwin's Black Box: The Biochemical Challenge to Evolution* (New York: The Free Press, 1996), in Tom Woodward, "Meeting Darwin's Wager," *Christianity Today* 41, no. 5, pt. 2 (28 April 1997): 14. Found at www.apologetics.org/articles/wager2.html.

17. Behe, *Darwin's Black Box*, quoted in Woodward, "Meeting Darwin's Wager." Found at www.apologetics.org/articles/wager1.html.

18. Sir Frederick Hoyle, "Hoyle on Evolution," *Nature* 294, no. 5837 (12 November 1981): 148. Quoted in Loughran, "Evolution?" Found at http://atschool.eduweb.co.uk/sbs777/vital/evolutio.html.

19. Behe, *Darwin's Black Box*, quoted in Woodward, "Meeting Darwin's Wager." Found at www.apologetics.org/articles/wager1.html.

20. William Paley, in Charles Colson, *Kingdoms in Conflict* (New York: William Morrow, 1987), 65.

21. A. E. Wilder-Smith, *The Natural Sciences Know Nothing of Evolution* (Costa Mesa, CA: T.W.F.T. Publishers, 1981), 82. In Hanegraaff, "Fat Chance." Found at www.equip.org/free/DC745.htm.

22. A. E. Wilder-Smith, *The Origin of Life,* vol. 3 (Gilbert, AZ: Eden Communications, 1983), videotape. In Hanegraaff, "Fat Chance." Found at www.equip.org/free/DC745.htm.

23. Miroslav Radman and Robert Wagner, "The High Fidelity of DNA Duplication," *Scientific America* 259, no. 2 (August 1988): 40-46. Quoted in Loughran, "Evolution?" Found at http://atschool.eduweb.co.uk/sbs777/vital/evolutio.html.

24. Stephen C. Meyer, "The Message in the Microcosm: DNA and the Death of Materialism" (1998). Found at www.windowview .org/ARNfiles/Message_in_the_Microcosm.html.

25. Charles B. Thaxton, Walter L. Bradley, and Robert L. Olsen, *The Mystery of Life's Origin: Reassessing Current Theories* (New York: New York Philosophical Library, 1984), 211-12. Quoted in Loughran, "Evolution?" Found at http://atschool.eduweb .co.uk/sbs777/vital/evolutio.html.

26. Phillip E. Johnson, *Darwin on Trial,* 2d ed. (Downers Grove, IL: InterVarsity, 1993), 111. Quoted in Strobel, *The Case for Faith: A Journalist Investigates the Toughest Objections to Christianity* (Grand Rapids: Zondervan, 2000), 104.

27. Gordon Rattray Taylor, *The Great Evolution Mystery* (New York: Harper & Row, 1983), 101-2. In Hanegraaff, "Fat Chance." Found at www.equip.org/free/DC745.htm.

28. Coppedge, *Evolution?* 218-20; Michael Denton, *Evolution: A Theory in Crisis* (Bethesda, MD: Adler & Adler, 1985), 332-33. In Hanegraaff, "Fat Chance." Found at www.equip.org/free/ DC745.htm.

29. Charles Darwin, *The Origin of Species,* quoted in Loughran, "Evolution?" Found at http://atschool.eduweb.co.uk/sbs777/ vital/evolutio.html.

30. Dr. Gary Parker, quoted in Loughran, "Evolution?" Found at http://atschool.eduweb.co.uk/sbs777/vital/evolutio.html.

31. Niles Eldredge, *Reinventing Darwin: The Great Debate at the High Table of Evolutionary Theory* (Hoboken, NJ: John Wiley & Sons, 1995), 95. Quoted in Genesis Park, "Abrupt Appearance in the Fossil Record." Found at www.genesispark.org/genpark/ abrupt/abrupt.htm.

32. J. Madeleine Nash, "When Life Exploded," *Time* 146, no. 23 (4 December 1995), cover. Quoted in Ray Bohlin, "Evolution's Big Bang" (Richardson, TX: Probe Ministries, 1996). Found at www.probe.org/docs/bigbang.html.

33. Nash, "When Life Exploded."

34. Stephen J. Gould, quoted in Nash, "When Life Exploded."

35. Samuel Bowring, quoted in Nash, "When Life Exploded."

36. Nash, "When Life Exploded."

37. Marvin Lubenow, *Bones of Contention: A Creationist Assessment of the Human Fossils* (Grand Rapids: Baker, 1992), 266. Quoted in Ray Bohlin, "Human Fossils: 'Just So' Stories of Apes and Humans" (1994). Found at www.probe.org/docs/hufossil.html.

38. Stephen Jay Gould, "The Return of Hopeful Monsters," *Natural History* 86, no. 6 (1977). Found at www.evolutionary .tripod.com/gould_nh_86_22-30.html.

39. H. S. Lipson, "A Physicist Looks at Evolution," *Physics Bulletin* 31 (1980): 138. Quoted in Brad Harrub, PhD, "Is Evolution Ready to Take Over Christianity?" (2003). Found at www .apologeticspress.org/inthenews/2003/itn-03-04.htm.

Chapter 7: America Is a Christian Nation

1. CNN Lawcenter, "Lawmakers Blast Pledge Ruling" (27 June 2002). Found at www.cnn.com/2002/LAW/06/26/pledge .allegiance.

2. Americans United for Separation of Church and State, "Colorado School District Unanimously Rejects Creationism in Science Classes" (10 April 2002). Found at www.au.org/press/ pr041002.htm.

3. Personal letter from Barry Lynn to Robert Jeffress on July 9, 1998.

4. David T. Moore, *Five Lies of the Century* (Wheaton, IL: Tyndale, 1995), 8, 11.

5. Delaware Constitution of 1776, Art. 22, quoted in Francis Newton Thorpe, ed., *The Federal and State Constitutions, Colonial Charters, and Other Organic Laws of the States, Territories, and Colonies Now and Heretofore Forming the United States of America,* 7 vols. (Washington, D.C.: Government Printing Office, 1909), 566. Found at http://press-pubs.uchicago.edu/ founders/documents/a6_3s2.html.

6. David Barton, *The Myth of Separation* (Aledo, TX: WallBuilder Press, 1992), 23.

7. Stephen McDowell and Mark Beliles, *America's Providential History* (Charlottesville, VA: Providence Press, 1989), 41.

8. James Capo, "One Nation—Under God?" *The Good News Magazine* (March/April 2001). Found at www.gnmagazine.org/ issues/gn33/nation.html.

9. Ken Woodward and David Gates, "How the Bible Made America," *Newsweek* (27 December 1982). Found at www.shakinand shinin.org/OurChristianHeritage-TheFoundingOfAmerica.html.

10. George Washington, quoted in W. Herbert Burk, *Washington's Prayers* (1907); William J. Johnson, *George Washington, the Christian* (New York: Abington Press, 1919), 24-35. Found at http://jagger.me.berkeley.edu/~lawton/gwprayer.html.

11. Inaugural address given by George Washington on April 30, 1789. Transcript of the National Archives and Records Administration. Found at www.archives.gov/exhibit_hall/american_originals/inaugtxt.html.

12. John Adams, quoted in Lester J. Capon, ed., *The Adams-Jefferson Letters,* vol. 2 (Chapel Hill, NC: University of North Carolina Press, 1959), 339-40.

13. Patrick Henry, quoted in Steve C. Dawson, *God's Providence in American History* (Rancho Cordova, CA: Steve C. Dawson, 1988).

14. John Quincy Adams, quoted in Billy Falling, *The Political Mission of the Church* (Valley Center, CA: Billy Falling Publishing, 1990), 40.

15. The Rutherford Institute, interview with Daniel Dreisbach, author of *Thomas Jefferson and the Separation Between Church and State* (New York: New York University Press, 2003). Found at www.rutherford.org.

16. Thomas Jefferson, quoted in Merrill D. Peterson, ed., *Jefferson Writings* (New York: Literary Classics of the United States, 1989), 510. Also found at http://religiousfreedom.lib.virginia.edu/sacred/danbury_1802.html.

17. Roger Williams, *Mr. Cottons Letter Lately Printed, Examined and Answered* (London, 1644), in Reuben Aldridge Guild, ed., *The Complete Writings of Roger Williams,* vol. 1 (New York: Russell & Russell, 1963), 108; William Sierichs Jr., "Ye Olde Walls of Separation," *Freethought Today* (March 2001). Found at www.ffrf.org/fttoday/march01/sierichs.html.

18. Larry Witham, "Church, State 'Wall' Not Idea of Jefferson," *The Washington Times* (5 August 2002). Found at www.washington times.com.

19. Thomas Jefferson, quoted in McDowell and Beliles, *America's Providential History,* 148; Barton, *The Myth of Separation,* 176.

20. *Runkel v. Winemiller,* 4 Harris and McHenry 276, 288 (Sup. Ct. Md., 1799), quoted in Barton, *The Myth of Separation,* 64.

21. *Church of the Holy Trinity v. U.S.* 143 U.S. 457, 469-470 (1892), quoted in Edwin S. Gaustad, *Faith of Our Fathers* (San Francisco: Harper & Row, 1987); Barton, *The Myth of Separation,* 48.

22. *The People v. Ruggles* 8 Johns 545 (Sup. Ct. N.Y., 1811), quoted in *Church of the Holy Trinity v. U.S.,* 143 U.S. 470-471 (1892); Barton, *The Myth of Separation,* 50.

23. Moore, *Five Lies,* 23.

24. *Vidal v. Girard's Executors,* 43 U.S. 126, 132 (1844), quoted in Christian Defense Fund, "One Nation Under God" (1997). Found at www.leaderu.com/orgs/cdf/onug/decisions.html.

25. *Vidal v. Girard's Executors,* quoted in Christian Defense Fund, "One Nation Under God." Found at www.leaderu.com/orgs/cdf/onug/decisions.html.

26. *The New England Primer* (Boston, 1777). Found at http://my.voyager.net/~jayjo/primer.htm.

27. Daniel Dreisbach, quoted in Witham, "Church, State 'Wall' Not Idea of Jefferson." Found at www.washingtontimes.com.

28. Philip Hamburger, quoted in Witham, "Church, State 'Wall' Not Idea of Jefferson." Found at www.washingtontimes.com.

29. Justice Clarence Thomas and Justice Antonin Scalia, quoted in Witham, "Church, State 'Wall' Not Idea of Jefferson." Found at www.washingtontimes.com.

30. *Engle v. Vitale,* 370 U.S. 421, 422 (1962), quoted in Barton, *The Myth of Separation,* 145.

31. *Engle v. Vitale,* 370 U.S. 421, 425, 430 (1962), quoted in Barton, *The Myth of Separation,* 146.

32. *Engle v. Vitale,* 370 U.S. 431 (1962), quoted in Barton, *The Myth of Separation,* 146.

33. *State Board of Education v. Board of Education Netcong,* 262 A.2d 21, 23 (Sup. Ct. N.J. 1970), in Barton, *The Myth of Separation,* 156.

34. *Abington School Dist. v. Schempp,* 374 U.S. 203 (1963). Found at http://caselaw.lp.findlaw.com/scripts/getcase.pl?navby=search &court=US&case=/us/374/203.html.

35. Thomas Jefferson, quoted in Herbert Lockyer, *Last Words of Saints and Sinners* (Grand Rapids: Kregel, 1968), 98; Barton, *The Myth of Separation,* 150.

36. *Grove v. Mead School District,* 753 F.2d 1528, 1540 (9th Cir. 1985), *cert. denied* 474 U.S. 826. In Barton, *The Myth of Separation,* 180-81.

37. *The People v. Ruggles,* 8 Johns. 545 (1811), quoted in Barton, *The Myth of Separation,* 56-57.

38. *DeSpain v. Dekalb County Community School District,* 384 F.2d 655, 836 (N.D. Ill. 1967), *cert. denied* 390 U.S. 906 (1967). Quoted in Barton, *The Myth of Separation,* 159.

39. *DeSpain v. Dekalb County Community School District,* 384 F.2d 841 (N.D. Ill. 1967), quoted in Barton, *The Myth of Separation,* 160.

40. George Washington, quoted in *The Massachusetts Centinel* (14 October 1789). Found at www.leaderu.com/humanities/ washington-thanksgiving.html.

41. *Stone v. Graham,* 449 U.S. 39 (1980). Found at http://caselaw
.lp/findlaw.com/scripts/getcase.pl?court=US&vol=449&invol=39.

42. William J. Bennett, *The Index of Leading Cultural Indicators:
Facts and Figures on the State of American Society* (New York:
Simon & Schuster, 1994), cited in Bennett, "Quantifying Amer-
ica's Decline," *Wall Street Journal* (15 March 1993).

43. Narconon Southern California, "Teen Alcoholism." Found at
www.alcoholism2.com/teen-alcoholism.htm.

44. Coalition Against Gun Violence, "Teen Gun Deaths." Found at
www.sbcoalition.org/articles/article.asp?Article=10.

45. Statistics on the total number of teenage abortions and the ages
of women who have had abortions from 1972–2000 came from
The Alan Guttmacher Institute and the U.S. Centers for Disease
Control and Prevention, respectively. Quoted in The Alan
Guttmacher Institute, "U.S. Teenage Pregnancy Statistics with
Comparative Statistics for Women Aged 20–24" (19 February
2004). Found at www.guttmacher.org/pubs/teen_stats.html.

46. Chief Justice Earl Warren, quoted in "Breakfast in Washington,"
Time 63, no. 7 (15 February 1954): 49.

Becoming a Velvet-Covered Brick

1. Paul E. Little, *How To Give Away Your Faith* (Downers Grove,
IL: InterVarsity, 1966), 32.

2. Arthur Burns, quoted in Os Guiness, *The Call: Finding and
Fulfilling the Central Purpose of Your Life* (Nashville: Word,
1998), 106.